1

MW00532421

The Call of the Spectacled Owl
An Artist's Journey through History, the Amazon, and Spirit (with Travel Tips)

By Patricia Robin Woodruff

To Scott,
I hope you enjoy
traveling along with
us on our adventure!
Love,
Patricia Robin Woodruff

First Edition
On-Demand Publishing, LLC

Summary: A thoughtful travelogue of spiritual artist, Patricia Robin Woodruff and her photographer daughter, Coriander in the Amazon jungle, Iquitos and Lima, Peru; delightful observations on the animals, plants, native earth religions, shamanism, ethnobotany, and history.

This book is dedicated to my children:

Cameron, my imaginative, wildly creative son,

Natty, my little angel, &

Coriander, my inspiring, born leader.

The Call of the Spectacled Owl: An Artist's Journey through History, the Amazon, and Spirit (with Travel Tips)

Tuesday: Our Night Flight to South America

Coriander eagerly leans forward to look out the small window, as the plane moves slowly down the dark runway. Suddenly my breath is caught with the exciting feeling as the plane accelerates, and my heart beats quicker, the runway lights flash by faster and faster until the deafening roar mellows and I know the plane is in its element. Looking down, I see the cars in orderly rows glittering in parking lot lights. All the buildings dwindle to doll houses in seconds until it all becomes just shimmering jewels forming unreadable, arcane symbols in the velvet black. My daughter curls up like a little dormouse, snuggled into her pillow with her rainbow stockinged feet in my lap. She looks much younger than her twenty-one years. Her auburn hair is spilling and curling into rivulets against the gently vibrating curve of the womb-like hull. Tomorrow morning we'll be in Lima, Peru.

Wednesday: Arriving at Iquitos - The Amazon River - An Amazonian Wildlife Park - Visiting Monkey Island

We have been traveling for ten hours, only one more hour to go. We find our flight in Lima and board a smaller Star Peru flight to Iquitos, our doorway to the jungle. As we buckle in, Coriander observes, "I swear these seats on the plane get smaller every time I travel." I laugh and say, "I'm sure most travelers feel that way!"

In our row, sitting next to the window, is a long and lanky fellow with a kind smile, who introduces himself as Frank. He says he grew up in Australia, but used to live in London where he met his wife and they both moved back to Australia (which explains his delicious accent.)

Our snacks on this commuter flight are pure carb/gluten: an un-iced cupcake and a roll. Coriander is sitting in the middle, with me on one side and Frank on the other. It's comical to see us both handing her our snack boxes at the same time because neither of us can eat gluten. I explain I have an auto-immune reaction to gluten. He explains that he is observing a strict vegetable/no-gluten diet because he is going to a week-long ayahuasca retreat for the second time.

I am excited to hear he knew about the traditional spiritual medicine of ayahuasca. I said, "Our tour company includes one night of the ayahuasca ceremony with a shaman, but they weren't intense about any dietary restrictions or anything."

I explain that I am an artist and I had heard about the ayahuasca ceremony about twenty years ago.
"What really fascinates me," I say, "Is that different people after drinking it, wind up having the same sort of visions. I read this article where they wound up painting images of the same thing. It seems to me

to be a way to tap into the Collective Unconscious. Since my artwork is mainly about Spirit and I try to touch on common images and archetypes, I'm really intrigued by this." Turning to Frank, I ask, "So what was your experience with it?"

Frank says that last time he participated in an ayahuasca ceremony, it gave him this amazing feeling of connection with the world. He looks at us very earnestly as he tells us he had a lung condition that was cured through the ritual. He says, "You know it makes you vomit, right?" I nod and he adds, "Since I was a kid, I've always had this problem with my respiratory system. Well, during that purging process, I felt like I was coughing up a hard walnut. I meant it really hurt! But afterwards I could breathe better than I had in the past fifteen years! It's really amazing. When I went back to the doctor, he said that the problem in my lungs had cleared up."

Coriander says that she hasn't decided if she wants to go through it or not because she hates throwing up. I agree but add that it just seems like everything has been pointing in this direction for me, so I was definitely doing it. I am just glad Coriander is able to hear about another experiences to be able to make an informed decision.

At that moment, through a break in the clouds we can see the magnificent Andes mountains, the rocky rugged peaks dusted with white snow. "Look, look!" I say excitedly to Coriander, pointing out the window at these impressive mountains. Since Frank has the window seat, I hand him my camera and he kindly takes a photo out of the window for me. We won't be seeing any more of these amazing mountains, since we will be down in the jungle in the Amazon basin. I think wistfully of visiting the sacred Incan site of Machu Picchu, but that will have to wait for some future trip.

I begin thinking of my spiritual journey, as I stare absentmindedly at the vinyl airplane seat in front of me. Since I was five years old in Sunday school classes, I knew that the religion I was being raised in didn't fit me. I had far too many questions and felt a deep dissatisfaction with the answers they gave me, especially the reply to just "take it on faith." This was important to me, because I could feel a deep connection to Spirit in every glorious sunset and awesome wonder in every uncurling flower, but I couldn't feel anything like that in the hollow words of men gone by.

Yet, when I stumbled across the poetry of Rabindranath Tagore stating, "The same stream of life that runs through my veins night and day, runs through the world and dances in rhythmic measures. It is the same life that shoots in joy through the dust of the earth in numberless blades of grass and breaks into tumultuous waves of leaves and flowers." I could feel an answering wave of affirmation. Inside, I could feel this strong connection to this god-force that created us all, and as I was continually called to become an artist, I felt like I was participating in that creative force.

I finally found a spiritual home at Four Quarters Interfaith Sanctuary of Earth Religions in Pennsylvania, where they are building a circle of standing stones. Here I could participate in ceremony with others who felt a deep connection to this creative force that we found in nature. My partner Woody and our kids, Cameron and Coriander, loved camping at the site, chatting with other kindred spirits, swimming in the fresh mountain waters, enjoying the music and fire circles with people who also felt this spiritual connection with the earth.

Although I studied many different religious books and teachings, it held no weight compared to the intense spiritual experiences in sweat lodge, in dreams,

and in ritual that connected me to my
path.

In my work as an artist, I felt the call to
remind people of the beauty of this world
and our connection to it. A present day
philosopher, Will Bason stated, "Artists
are the shamans of our time." This rang
true to me, since the process of art is to
bring emotions and images from the
invisible world of spirit into the visible
world. The term of shaman originates in
Siberia and means, "one who knows." I
wanted to find out more on how those
ancient priestesses and shamans
connected to Spirit. I wanted to "know."

So throughout the past twenty years, I
have been learning about ancient religions
that explore connections to the earth. I
have been blessed with the opportunity
to visit a variety of ancient sacred sites. I
have watched the dawning sun on the
spring equinox shine upon ancient Celtic
writing marking the pagan rites of spring,
and visited the locations of many sacred

Native American sites. I have explored aspects of the ancient Norse religion in Oslo, Norway, and spent several months around the Mediterranean area visiting cathedrals and museums. I have stood under the huge temple columns dedicated to the Roman gods and goddesses, and explored a secret underground temple to Mithras, dipping my hand in the sacred spring water. I have entered the 6,000 year-old tombs on the island of Malta, and walked in the oldest free-standing temples in the world dedicated to an ancient earth fertility goddess. Now my daughter and I would be traveling to the land held sacred by Pachamama, the great Earth Mother.

My thoughts return to the present as we touch down briefly in Cusco, the ancient ruling city at the time of the Incan Empire. We wish Frank well as he disembarks this commuter flight for his retreat. After taking on some more passengers, we're off to the town of Iquitos on the banks of the Amazon river.

Iquitos

After thirteen hours of planes and airports we are finally in Iquitos. It has the amazing distinction of being the largest town in the world that has no roads going into it. This was because it was built during the Rubber Boom and all the transportation was along the Amazon River, but they needed a headquarters deep in the jungle. In the present day, Iquitos is also accessible by plane, which is definitely quicker than the average week-long boat trip up the Amazon from Lima. The airport is one steamy open-air room where we wait for Coriander's bag that had been checked.

I'll blame my mistake on hardly sleeping during our red-eye flight, but when a man comes over to me and asks in a heavy accent, "Manti?" I say yes, thinking he is from the tour company. He gathers up our bags and pushes the cart through the exit, handing the guard our bits of paper that proves they are our bags. As we step outside, we come across the fellow who is supposed to pick us up and he has a sign with our name on it. I realize that the first fellow is one of those hangers-on at the airport who make a quick buck off of tourists. However, he had helpfully loaded our bags and pushed them out to the parking lot, so I give him a two dollar tip and quickly hop into our car. It is hot and steamy and the car has most definitely seen better days. Not only does it not have air conditioning, but the front dash is battered enough that I'm not sure any of the controls work, but apparently this is not an issue in Iquitos.

The town of Iquitos is a chaotic place and we enter a mad clap of sensations! A blur of mopeds, carts built onto motorcycles (our driver called them "motorcars" when I ask what they are, but in Thailand they are called the more onomatopoeic name of tuk-tuks.) Being tossed into the humid heat and the wild ride of traffic, makes me feel like I am damp laundry tumbling in the dryer. The roar of traffic is deafening! While the road is often marked two lanes for cars, apparently this doesn't apply to three-wheeled tuk-tuks or to motorcycles. They can generally fit about three and a half tuk-tuks across or approximately seven motorcycles or any combination thereof and when things get tight, a motorcycle or tuk-tuk might nonchalantly use the oncoming traffic lane or sidewalk. Vehicles generally stop for the occasional red light, but after that, it seems anything goes!

The houses are a huge scrap collage leaning sadly against each other for mutual support. There are re-used iron grates on doors, rough-cut lumber (sometimes half-heartedly painted), thatched palm roofs next to corrugated steel roofs looking like they've been scavenged and re-used many times, with a rare shiny, sleek window glass, and aluminum building looking like an alien space building that materialized there. In my mind, I find myself paraphrasing the quote from the comedy, Blazing Saddles, "We don't need no stinkin' ...car inspections, traffic regulations, building regulations, etc."

We finally stop at the office for our tour company. Getting shakily out of the battered old car and stepping into a room that would have been a great set for a third-world interrogation room in a Humphrey Bogart movie; a wrought iron grating on the door, and high cement walls covered in an odd assortment of tattered posters, and a large area map. Unlike the foreign police in the old movies, the folks are smiling and friendly (and better than that... give us the password to their wifi!) Coriander sends quick text messages to family to let them know we are here and safe, while I pay the balance on our reservations.

We are introduced to our tour guide, Ashuco; not tall, but weathered, brown, wiry and strong with a reassuring air of competency. He hefts both our bags onto his shoulders and whisks us back out into the battered car. A short drive later and we are at a bustling dock and squeezing our way through a busy little market. The rows of fish and fowl, bright vegetables and fruit, the chatter and smells form a busy blur. One image that stands out is a snack seller with fat shish-ka-bobbed grubs as big as your thumb, golden, and toasted on sticks. The vague thought of, "I should get a photo of this," gets lost in trying to keep my balance now that we are walking on a make-shift walkway of boards and logs that lead down to a floating building with a tall palm-thatched roof. Once on board, it appears to be a floating bar room with tables and posters of drinks, empty in the middle of the day. Tethered to this is a long, shallow boat, with a roof in the middle (also thatched with palm leaves) and benches underneath. I find out later the boat is called a "pecamari." We gratefully sit down on the bench cushions in the shade under the roof and Ashuco takes care of getting our luggage carefully on board. Although I brought a portable water filter with me, I am reassured to see him load on seven large carboys of bottled water. A weathered old boatman with few teeth and fewer words, motors us out onto the Amazon river.

Floating bar in Iquitos

Our guide, Ashuco Perez, is part Spanish and part native Indian. While it takes us a while to get used to his heavy accent, we enjoy hearing him tell about the Amazon and its inhabitants. He smiles easily and often, which reveals his glimmering gold tooth.

I am curious, especially with his Amerindian heritage, what his experience has been in spiritual matters and what the ayahuasca ceremony is like. I had only heard that it was a sacred ceremony under the guidance of a shaman, where participants drink a special brew of plants and the ayahuasca vine and they would have visions. A friend had participated in a ceremony and told me about her experiences. She explained that the common drawback of vomiting after taking the potion is Spirit's way of purging out past traumas and illness out of your body. She said she had an amazing experience of being in touch with a powerful grandmother-type figure, felt an amazing connection with the Universe, and afterwards seen a marked improvement with her childhood asthma.

Ashuco explains that in the tribe he grew up in the shaman doesn't usually do the ayahuasca. They do a ritual involving a "bite" from a poison dart frog to give them lots of energy. The poison dart frog is native to Central and South America and there are numerous varieties of the species.

Later I researched the ritual of kambo, which Ashuco was referring to. It's not actually a bite, but instead the first layer of skin is burnt with a smoldering stick and then the "poison" is introduced to the wound. This is collected by the shaman and harvested from the giant leaf frog (Phyllomedusa bicolor) by gently pinioning the frog and "tickling" its sides. The frog secretes a white fluid that is gathered on a stick and then the frog is released.

The ritual of kambo is said to have originated from an ancient shaman whose people were struck down with a strange disease. When all that he had tried had failed, the shaman took ayahuasca and it guided him on how to administer the ritual of kambo to cure his tribe.

This secretion has been studied by various scientists and it has been found to contain peptides that stimulate the immune system. It actually has antibiotic properties as well.

The people that practice the ritual of kambo believe it gives the participant a keenness of eye, increased strength and special hunting powers. It is given to members of the tribe that are considered lazy, as a "cure." It also produces a purging process to get rid of the body's ills. Some users experience a euphoric, dream-like state which can be very valuable in terms of psycho-spiritual development.

Ashuco counts up the tiny freckle-like scars on his muscled inner forearm.

"Seeks or seven time," he states with a smile. "Geeve lots of energy! I am fifty. Am strong. De frog poison do eet. Ees quick. Five, ten meenutes. De ayahuasca ceremony take more time. Dese, five meenutes. Give me lots of energy!" Certainly we had examples of this all through the week; when he easily carried several heavy bags all at once or when we had hiked for over an hour, he found we had forgotten something and trotted back to the village and back again in only forty minutes all together!

I really want to talk more about his spirituality but he seems reticent on the subject, although he says that, yes, they believe in the spirits of nature. He explains that the anaconda is the spirit of the Amazon. He calls it "matatoro," which I find out later means, "killer or death of bulls." He identifies our little wizened boatman as the shaman who will be conducting our ayahuasca ceremony later in the week, although I didn't find out until later that Ashuco was studying to become a shaman trained in ayahuasca.

Coriander has been looking all around around us as the boat motors up the Amazon. She leans over and remarks to me, "I didn't think the Amazon river would be so wide! I guess in the movies I've watched they were all traveling up tributaries, so it looked like a narrow river with the jungle hanging over it." Ashuco explains that we aren't even in the wet season when it gets even wider!

We can see the high banks of mud on the side of the river, rising up about twenty or thirty feet (about nine meters) and he explains that during the wet season, the river will cover that and flood inland. Later on, I looked it up in Wikipedia and it said, "The width of the Amazon is between 1.6 and 10 kilometers (1.0 and 6.2 miles) at low stage, but expands during the wet season to 48 kilometers (30 miles) or more." At this point all I know is that it is *really* wide and muddy-brown and amazing. I put my arm over the shallow edge of the boat and my fingertips can just touch the warm water. I anoint my brow like a blessing.

Scattered along the banks of the river, we see a little cluster of long canoes, then a longer boat like our pecamari, with a palm roof tethered up at the riverbank to long sticks sunk into the mud. Next to it is a make-shift staircase climbing the steep hill only to disappear into the tall grasses at the top. Ashuco explains with a sweep of his arm, "Dese is rice. All dese. Rice. Dey grow de food for de village."

After about an hour, our boatman turns towards a steep staircase on the shore. Ashuco turns to us and explains, "We see de animals. Lots of animals here." He indicates that we should just leave our bags on the boat and we follow him up the makeshift steps cut into the steep bank. At the top of the river bank we start following a grassy path, passing lovely blooming flowers in all the colors of

the rainbow. Ashuco leads us along to
what seems to be a little open air zoo.

I feel like I am trying to look everywhere
at once! Above me I can see green round
fruit that look like limes, although Ashuco
calls them "limons" and in front of me I
recognize a mango tree. To my left is a
large pond covered in gigantic waterlilies,
while off to my right up a small hill
appears to be a cheerily painted tree
house rising up, with a brightly colored
macaw who stands grandly on a branch at
the top, lord of the manor! After spotting
the treehouse, Coriander quickly starts
climbing. She slows down as she
approaches the macaw.
"I don't know, Ma!" she calls down. "He's
not looking happy with me being up here."
"I'm sure you'll be fine," I reassure her.
"Get his picture," I add.
"I don't know," she says dryly. "What if
he doesn't want his picture taken? It
might make him crankier. He might bite
my camera. You know he has an awful big
beak."

Smiling, I shake my head at her silliness as she climbs up the rest of the way and looks around, taking several photos of the blue and yellow macaw.

When she descends, I take my turn climbing the treehouse and the bird turns his head sideways to look at me beadily, squawking and sidling along the branch. He seems to say, "You may be bigger, but I am descended from a mighty line of dinosaurs and don't you forget it!"
I laughingly call down to her, "Alright," I say, "I can see where the macaw looks a lot more intimidating close up."

When we are both back on the ground, Ashuco leads us around to take a closer look at the ponds. One is fenced in with several turtles lounging about and two caimans enjoying the sun. I know they are a smaller cousin of an alligator and only about four feet long, but they still look like nothing I would want to get too close to. Their jaws are rather toothy and

intimidating even if they look deceptively
lazy and slow moving at the moment.

Ashuco points to a small heron standing
at the far edge of the pond, looking like a
compact version of a great blue heron.
"Ees a striated heron."
The gray-blue bird stands there, still as a
statue, looking intently into the dark
green depths of the pond, its dagger-like
beak poised to catch an unwary fish.

Ashuco beckons us across a narrow
grassy promontory, past a post which has
some huge, empty snail shells at its base,
and out onto a miniature island with an
octagonal tin-roofed gazebo. As we walk
to the other side of the gazebo, some
huge fish come swimming to the surface.

"They're gorgeous!" I exclaim.
Their scales are very distinctively diamond
shaped and glimmer pink and black in the
murky water. Their arched backs
undulate to the surface and back down,

so it's hard to see their whole length, but they seem almost as large as a person.

"Ees a paiche," Ashuco says. "Ees a big fish. Dey can get as beeg as four meeters."

"Four meters?! That's like... like thirteen feet long, but I guess these are more like five feet long."

I could certainly see this huge fish could be one of the origins of mermaid stories, but instead of a pretty woman's face, it had a large wide mouth and sad eyes that reminded me of a begging puppy dog. He seemed to be asking for treats we didn't have. I got down on my hands and knees to get a closer look at this beautiful fish.

"Careful there, Ma," warned Coriander, clutching her camera. "He'll take a bite out of you."

"No, he won't. Can you get a photo of his scales?" I asked. "I really want to draw him when I get home."

She was actually more correct than I knew at the time, since after I looked it up, they do feed on small land mammals that get too close to the edge of the water, as well as smaller fish and crustaceans. But when no food was forthcoming, he shrugged sadly off into the depths of the pond.

We saw another fish eagerly swim over to us, not wanting to miss any treats being passed out. This one was a rather circular flat fish, swimming about like a vertical dinner plate.
"Dese is a pacu. Pacu. Related to de piranha," Ashuco tells us.

I look out along the pond which is thick with partially submerged bamboo and covered in large water lilies. I find out later that these water lilies are named Victoria Regis after the English Queen, and they are pretty impressive indeed! The pads are supported by a network of veins underneath that are filled with air and the large ones can even support the weight of a person. They aren't bothered by the rising waters of the Amazon, because their stems can keep on growing to about twenty feet long (six meters) and the pads can grow to eight feet across! But what I found really cool about them is that the lily flowers change sex. When they first bloom in the evening, they are white and female, smelling sweetly of pineapple that attracts the local scarab beetles. The beetles climb in there at night and hang out, then the flower shuts up near the break of day, turning into a male, pollen-producing flower that coats the bugs with pollen. During this time, the lily flower changes color to a dark pink which doesn't attract the scarab beetle like the white blossoms do. It then re-opens the next night, and the bug flies off to find another white flower and winds up pollinating it.

When we walk back onto our grass "bridge," Ashuco points up at a large blue-gray hawk circling above.
"Dese is de snail kite," he said. "De hawk, he eats de snails," pointing down at the pile of empty snail shells at the base of the post. I can see where that sunlit post

might be a favorite seat for a raptor to have dinner on. The dark form of the snail kite soars on above us, reveling in the updraft of the warming afternoon.

Paiche

This was a nice break traveling up the Amazon river. We get back in the boat and it takes us about another hour motoring upstream before we get to our camp. Along the way we had passed some construction on the shore and some large steel boats that actually had cranes and backhoe scoops on them. When we asked about that, Ashuco explained that it was hydroelectric being built, which I found a little more reassuring than the big oil tankers that we passed.

Our long boat pulls up next to an uprooted tree and a few mooring sticks sunk deep in the silty mud. Ashuco nimbly leaps out and quickly ties up the boat. He reaches out to help us out onto the stiff mud. "I get de bags. You no worry," he says as he loads both of our suitcases onto his shoulders, as well as his own backpack and climbs the steep cliff with ease. I follow at a slower pace, carefully stepping onto the sun stiffened clay, and onto a long board with thin runners nailed across it to provide traction. This horizontal ladder gets us to a series of log and plank steps that let us finally crest the steep bank of the Amazon. My view opens up onto a small rice field that is in the process of being harvested by hand. The ripe and golden tasseled heads hang down with the weight of the grain. Nearby are small "hay stacks" of the cut stalks that are drying in the mid-day sun. In the distance, I can see a man in a broad brimmed hat cutting down the stalks and piling them up.

We walk along the beaten path following Ashuco, coming to thicker vegetation and our path becomes a small boardwalk. Literally. It is made of rough-cut boards, raised off the mud by logs underneath. In some places, someone had added a bamboo railing on one side to hang on to. The foliage briefly opens out into a clearing with a storage hut on one side of us and what looks like an open air house on the other side, set back into the trees and bushes.

The storage hut is raised up on pilings, with a wooden floor, but not much in the way of walls. The roof is the same woven palm branches that thatched our little boat roof. Our plank road continues on past the hut, eventually turning into a short bridge over a small brown waterway with the bamboo railing on one side to help us across. The boards are springy under our step. It is mildly unnerving, but it all holds up as we cross. Our walk into camp takes us about fifteen minutes but finally, we come to the end.

In front of us are several small huts in a rectangle formation around a clearing full of small plantings. Little stepping stones made of slices of tree trunks wend around the clearing. Ashuco leads us straight to a raised hut where we are to stay the rest of the week. There we are greeted by another young Peruvian man, who says in almost unaccented English, "Welcome to the jungle." There are steps up to a narrow front porch. We take off our muddy shoes on the small porch as Ashuco places our luggage in the room.

Our cabins are actually roofed with corrugated sheet steel. As I go inside and look around, I notice that the large open windows are all screened in, with privacy curtains hanging all around the room. The accommodations are simple but neat. We have three wooden beds, two are made up for us and the other is a bare mattress. Our young man asks if it is good, the way things are made up and we assure him it is just fine. Ashuco lets us know that our late lunch is going to be at 3 PM in the large screened-in hut at the far corner of the clearing and they leave us to unpack. As I put my suitcase on the bare mattress, Coriander starts giggling at the whole unreality of our experience, "I didn't expect to be greeted by a Guns & Roses song," she says laughingly.

The square room has a bare plank floor. There is a table that we promptly put our toiletries stuff on and in one corner of the room it is sectioned off into bathroom space: an open shower stall at the end (with no curtain), a toilet in the middle (with no seat), and a small sink closest to the door. Ashuco had mentioned that the water in camp was not drinkable. It is taken from the Amazon river, and although filtered, it is still rather brown. I was steamed enough from the walk that I didn't care. Peeling off my sweaty clothes I promptly jump under the shower. It is odd to find no adjustment for temperature. The controls are only on or off for the cold shower, but the cool feels delicious and I linger under the shower for a while. Coriander follows after me, but is much quicker since she's always been sensitive to cold water. When she gets out she teases me, "I think that's the only time in my life, you've taken a longer shower than me!" We had just enough time to lie down and rest our eyes before our late lunch.

It may have been all the hiking, or it may have been that I hadn't had anything to eat since 4 AM on the plane and that was a small jello fruit cup, but the fish they serve is delicious! It is served with a healthy helping of rice, some crispy fried banana pieces (which Coriander falls in love with and promptly steals some of mine), and a side of sliced cucumbers and tomatoes that seem like they are salted. I find it a very refreshing dish. Ashuco joins us, "Hungry?!" he asks with a grin, eyeing up Coriander who had already finished half her plate.

"Yes, I'm always hungry," she replies. Her slender build seeming to contradict her words.

"She just burns it off," I explain.

Ashuco says that the fish is pacu, the round plate-like fish we had seen that morning.

"After lunch, we go to Monkey Island, yes?" he asks.

"Absolutely," said Coriander, her eyes glowing in anticipation.

"Are we the only ones here right now?" I
ask, since the huge screened-in dining hall
is empty except for us.
"Yes. We get more people tomorrow.
Now dere is just you."

It feels very neat to have the whole place
to ourselves! Feeling special, we fill up
our water bottles at the drinking water
cooler and go back outside. Ashuco leads
us along the "stepping stones" out past
the hammock room (a screened in room
that had about twenty hammocks hanging
from the ceiling beams) and we follow the
boardwalk back down to the boat to go to
Monkey Island (but I make them stop
once or twice so I can get a photo of a
flitting butterfly on the railing or the
nearby bushes.) We pass a woman doing
laundry down at the riverbank. She has
put her tub of laundry in her canoe and
we watch as she dips the clothes into the
river, rubs it with soap, and rinses it back
out in the brown river, finally wringing it
out and putting it into her laundry tub,

which I suppose she will haul home to
hang on a laundry line in the sun.

Maniti Camp

Our little wizened boatman motors us back down the river and then crosses the wide expanse to the other side. We continue along the Amazon and turn up a tributary, where we dock and climb the shallow set of steps. We follow Ashuco as he leads us across a wide field and some makeshift boardwalks with bamboo railings built over a marshy area.

I marvel at the flitting, jewel-like dragonflies dancing all around us. I just have to stop on the boardwalk to take some photos of some of the flitting dragonflies and a glorious red butterfly perched on a lily pad. The dragonflies make me pause in thought, their shimmering wings reminding me of my connection to Spirit. I recall a vivid memory of standing in the stream at my spiritual home of Four Quarters Interfaith Sanctuary in PA, and having the shining creatures land gently on my arms like blessings; one of those golden moments of summer when I felt entirely connected to the natural world. I still had three silver dragonflies woven into a thin braid of my hair to remind me of my connection to All.

"C'mon, Ma!" Coriander called, "We're never going to get anywhere if you keep stopping to take a picture of every butterfly."
"But they're pretty!" I protested, coming out of my silent reverie.
"For de Mom," said Ashuco, sticking up for me, "Let her take her peecture." He explains while we are paused, "Dese monkeys are rescued monkeys," says Ashuco, "Some Indians steel eet de monkey meat and sell de babies as pets. Dese are rescued and brought to de island. Dese is a preserve. De monkeys live safe on de island."

I get my photo and the red butterfly flits off on its erratic aerial path, going about its mysterious butterfly business.
Curious, I ask Ashuco what "butterfly" is in Spanish.
"Mariposa," he replies.

"How pretty! Mariposa!" I say, repeating after him, so I can remember it better.

We continue on the path and come to a grassy clearing with a few tall trees where monkeys are playing. One promptly comes right down to us and Ashuco identifies it as a Capuchin monkey.
I mention to Coriander, "That's where you get cappuccino, because the drink is brown like the robes of the Capuchin monks. I'm sure he gets his name from his brown fur like the monk robes."
I kneel down to get a closer look at him, and as quick as a wink, he clambers up onto my shoulder and starts examining my hair. I can't help but laugh as he starts licking my neck. "Get a picture," I gasp to Coriander in between bouts of giggles.

He frolics around my shoulders for a bit, then climbs down, and scampers over to Coriander to check out her camera. By this time, one of the men who works there had come over and he coaxes the little monkey to climb up Coriander. Now I have a chance to take pictures of her as she starts laughing over her little monkey companion.

Our little brown monkey climbs down and starts to nibble a metal knob on Coriander's camera. She indulges him for a bit, and then shoos him away from it when he starts to bite harder.
Looking up at the fellow who works here, she asks, "What's his name?"
"King Kong" is the amusing answer.

Our miniature King Kong comes back over to me, picking up a large piece of bark and pressing it to my shin. It drops on the ground and I hand it back to him, noticing his tiny little hands with long clever fingers. He looks so darling, like a little wizened elf. He tries several times to stick the bark to the bare part of my shin below my shorts.

His behavior is amusing, but puzzling. I'm not sure if he thinks my legs should be covered up better or not. I crouch down to pass him the bark again and in a twinkling, he dashes off, just as I see my room key fall to the ground in front of me. I look over at him perched at a distance on a rock and he's holding a bit of bright plastic in his clever little hands and nibbling on it in an exploratory way.

That quick! he had unzipped my tummy pack, grabbed my miniature disposable tooth brush, and run off with it leaving the pocket unzipped. He knew he was in trouble when the keeper noticed his guilty movements and came after him.

King Kong surrenders his prize on the ground and scampers up the tree. The keeper picks up the tiny toothbrush and gives it back to me. I was only going to dispose of it anyway, and I'm simply relieved that my room key hadn't been snatched. From then on, I keep a guarding hand on my tummy pack and urge Coriander to do the same.

With King Kong's retreat to the trees, it gives me a chance to look at some of the other monkeys there. Ashuco points out the long-limbed spider monkeys that are hanging from the trees; angular and gawky like gangly teens after a growth spurt. One notices our attention is on him and he drops to the ground and lopes on over to us, taking my hand in a gentlemanly fashion. He walks sociably with me under the palms for a little bit before deciding to clamber back into the tree.

Pointing up further into the tree, Ashuco points out a tamarin. Its orange and black fur makes it stand out even though it is pretty high up. Another monkey wanders over to check us out. Apparently he is a young wooly monkey, which I find out later are highly endangered. His short fuzzy fur gives him a very soft appearance. He also decides to use us as a jungle gym and clambers around my shoulders and licks my arm.

"I wonder if they like the salt," I comment. "I've been sweating like crazy." But Coriander has no more idea than I do.

"I hope I sweated off my bug spray," I add, "I don't want to make the little guy sick." But he clambers happily down and goes over to chase another monkey around the base of the tree.

We had been slowly working our way closer to a thatched hut, but now Ashuco calls our attention off to the side, to an artificial pool of water that is fenced in with a low log fence. The keeper has fished out a nobbly-looking turtle and placed him on the ground for us to look at. I get down and examine this fascinating creature.

"Ees de matamata turtle. Ees prehistoric."
"It sure looks like it!" I agree.
The shell is dark and deeply ridged like a rough and ragged oyster shell, only he's about a half a meter long (about 20

inches.) The head is pretty big and looking large and out of proportion to the body; a wide neck with ridged flaps of skin coming to a triangular head ending in a thin, horny-looking snout. I can see where he would just look like a soggy lump of leaves in the marsh.

"Eet was rescued. Dey sell de matamata for lots of money as pets, de poachers," Ashuco tells us.

We look over at the man who works here who is poking around in the artificial pond with a long pole. Finally, he finds what he had been looking for and out of the murky water emerges a huge, dappled Anaconda!

I suppose in the greater scheme of things, this one *technically* is a small example of its species, I'd guess only about 10 feet long. An "average" length anaconda is about 20 feet (or 6 meters) and the longest was almost 28 feet long and weighing in at almost 500 pounds, earning it the title of heaviest snake in the world!

Although we had expressed squeamishness about meeting a tarantula, both Coriander and I have no problem with holding a huge snake. Emotionally at least... physically it is pretty heavy! The animal keeper indicates that we need to keep a tight grip on its neck and it is also still a bit muddy and slippery from the pond. Coriander excitedly scampers forward to hold it first, while I get a photo of her.

We switch places and I take the heavy length of snake in my arms, his muddy and muscular body moving slowly in my arms. I don't want to hold his neck too tightly in my grip, but I don't want him to get away either. His body is cool and damp from the swamp water and I ignore my arms and t-shirt getting muddy as an inconsequential part of this amazing experience. I can feel his powerful muscles pushing against my grip, his weight dragging me down. Time seems to stop, and I am filled with a deep understanding of why this animal would be the personified spirit of the Amazon river. Matatoro, the spirit guide of the watery subterranean world... the surging sinuous power of kundalini energy moving through the spine... the cosmic anaconda, whose skin patterns are said to hold all the patterns of the Universe, and where magical messages are written that are able to be interpreted by the shamans. Powerful, primordial, unstoppable, inexorable...

My awareness comes back to the real world as his heavy weight is lifted off of me by the animal keeper. The anaconda doesn't seem too annoyed at being dragged out of its home, but it has been strongly pushing to get back there, so I surrender it to the keeper, and he puts it back into the water. I stand there a moment, looking at the murky water, feeling awe as well as gratitude for the brief moment of understanding.

Ashuco beckons us over to a small group of people who are holding a sloth. When they finish, Coriander takes a turn and then I get to cuddle the cute little thing, his dark eyes looking bigger with the black mask of fur around them. His fur is a bit coarse, almost closer to hay than to hair, but he holds onto me like a baby and rests his adorable little face on my shoulder with a contented sigh. He slowly wraps his arms around me, while we walk back to the thatched hut.

With a delighted grin, Ashuco points out the tiny little monkeys scampering around the thatched roof.
"Dey squirrel monkeys. Leetle monkeys."
I could see where they get their name because they are just as tiny as little squirrels. Yet, they grab onto the roof beams with their tiny hands, and look at us with clever brown faces. They remind me of the stories of little Scottish brownies who will be running off in a minute to manufacture tiny shoes.

As we get to the hut, Ashuco warns us
that they are going to close soon. He
asks us if we want to try a free sample of
a drink they sell there.
"Eets roots, honey, jungle herbs. Eets
medicinal."

Coriander has just taken a gulp of her
little cup and says gasping, "And alcohol!"
I take a careful sip (without disturbing my
cute little companion sloth.) My eyes
widen. It is pretty powerful alcohol, all
right! At least we don't have to worry
about whether it is sterile or not. It has a
fascinating taste, with a touch of sweet,
and certainly a strange little tang of
herbs, but we pass on purchasing one of
the unlabeled plastic bottles of home
brew. I do dig some money out of my
tummy pack and give it to Coriander to
put into the donation box for the food
and care of the animals.

With the drink still drifting like warm
smoke in my stomach, I am sitting on the

bench with my adorable little sloth curled around me, when a mama squirrel monkey with an even tinier baby clinging to her back comes in. She scampers around the edges of the porch and a few people gather around to get a photo of her.

Finally, Ashuco says it is time to go. I reluctantly hand my sloth over to him and Ashuco gently tucks him up in the rafters. The sloth's long claws gently wrap around the beam, and he starts to slowly work his way upward with an air of philosophical resignation.

We retrace our steps. When we come to the little pond and the boardwalk over it, the sun is lowering, turning the pond to deep blues and golds. The dragonflies are flitting about like flying jewels and I impulsively fling my arms up to the sky with joy for such a beautiful day full of wonders!

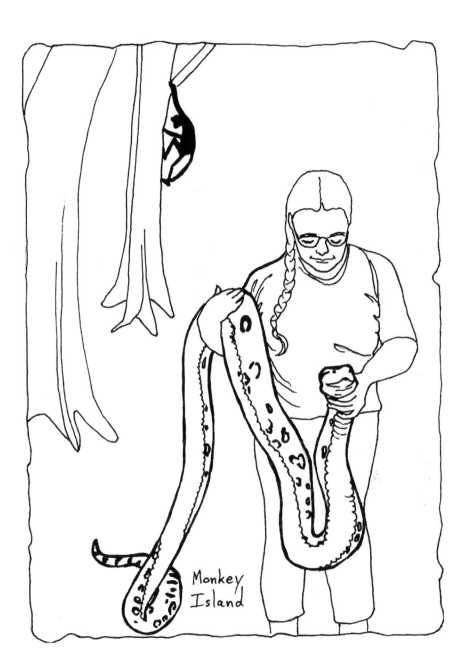

Monkey
Island

Our boatman takes us back to camp. It is a little trickier navigating our plank walkway back to the cabins in the failing light, but we manage. Ashuco lets us know that dinner is at 7 PM and by the time we get back the generator seems to be going because the light is on in our cabin. I get a quick rinse while Coriander goes to hang out in the hammock room for a bit. I join her and we wander over to the screened-in dining hut where the delicious scent of grilling chicken lures us in.

Ashuco enters the large screen-room after dinner, his nut brown face crinkles up into his familiar smile. "You hear dat?!" he asks excitedly about the haunting, descending whistle that we hear in the dark jungle outside. "Dat is de potoo. De potoo is related to de nightjar."

The trilling noises are, as we guessed, tree frogs. We hear a loud, deep "chuck-chuck-chuck" that Ashuco informs us is the bamboo rat.

"Wait a minute, wait a minute!" said Coriander, "Do you mean a rat rat? Or like a bird... you know... like the "snail kite" is a bird?"

"Ees a rat."

Her eyes widened. "No rat should be making a sound that big! Rats go squeak. How big is it?"

Ashuco measures it out with his hands, about a foot long.

"You know," stated Coriander dryly, "I'm really glad I don't have internet access right now and can't look up a picture!"

It's neat learning from Ashuco to recognize the animal calls. He makes many of the animal sounds so we can recognize them; the pallid dove calls with a soft mournful note like a bamboo flute, a chuffing noise that is the sound of the smaller nocturnal jungle rat, the trilling evening noise of the tiny frogs, the onomatopoeia of the chachalaca birds and the cuckoo, the tiny trill of the seed-eater bird and the booming sound of the spectacled owl.

At last, we walk back to our cabin in the dark. The mosquitos swiftly flock all around us. Coriander starts flapping her hands around to chase them away. Finally, getting really fed up, she starts frantically waving her hands all around her head and upper body, then froze. "Ohmigod!" she said, "The Macarena dance was invented to chase away mosquitos!" which makes us both dissolve into giggles.

Thursday: Jungle Walk - Ayahuasca Ceremony

I wake with the vague sensation of being in my tent at Four Quarters and hearing a Native American flute being played inexpertly in the distance. It finally registers on my groggy mind that, no, I am in the jungle and what I'm hearing is a bird call, not someone learning to play the flute. This must be the call of the pallid dove.

I feel revitalized after sleeping very soundly, only waking slightly when a storm blew through during the night, washing over me with beautiful cool air, and blowing our privacy curtains gently over my face. Now, with a solid twelve hours of sleep, I feel up to tackling the morning's hike. Coriander looks at me drowsily as I pull on my t-shirt and shorts. "I'll meet you over at breakfast," I say, and step out into the steamy warmth and bright sunlight. I hop merrily on the log "stepping stones" to avoid the mud from the brief rain last night.

Our screened-in dining hall is already starting to feel familiar and I help myself to lovely, fresh pineapple, and orange juice. After breakfast, on my way out the screen door, I notice a butterfly has trapped itself inside. It has beautiful black dashes on its wings and a splash of orange. I'm able to get in close and study it, looking at the little black dashes and feeling like Spirit has written a message of freedom there for me. I gently coax it out the door towards the open sky and follow it.

The rain last night has caused mushrooms to sprout all over, on all the "stepping logs" between the cabins, and the mud had gotten slippery on our path. Ashuco urges us to change our footwear to big, black rubber boots, waving us towards what looks like a huge crop of black mushrooms. The boots are placed upside down on sticks of bamboo set into the ground and the sizes are visible on the bottom of the sole. Coriander and I wander amid this strange crop and pick out sizes that fit us.

When we clump over to the guides' cabin in our big rubber boots, Ashuco is sitting on his cabin steps and sharpening his machete in a business-like manner. Looking up with a grin, he hops up, and leads us down our path made of logs and rough-cut boards out to the banks of the river.

Our weathered old boatman is already there. He nimbly hops down on the muddy bank and offers his strong, gnarled hand to steady us climbing onto the bow of the pecamari. He motors us down the muddy Amazon, recognizing landmarks that all sort of blur for me; one makeshift log and lumber staircase up the muddy cliffs looking much like another. We cross the broad expanse of the river to the "lowland" side and disembark to follow a path up to a small village.

There, as incongruous as the Yellow Brick Road through the forest of Oz, is a raised cement sidewalk. Following it takes us past various houses built up on poles. Standing as gawky as teenagers in ragged blue jeans, the houses are made of rough cut lumber, thatched with palms with the peak of the roof capped with corrugated sheet steel. Long-legged chickens meander under the pilings and snuggle into hollows they've made in the bare dirt under the house. Ashuco waves and exchanges pleasantries with some men weaving thatching for a roof.

We are joined on our hike by two scrawny black and white dogs that quietly accompany us.
"Ashuco?" asks Coriander, "What's a good jungle name for a dog?"
"Dog," he replies absentmindedly, waving to another villager.
Dissatisfied with that answer, Coriander takes matters into her own hands and promptly dubs them Mosquito and Lydia.

We discover the spot where the poet, Shel Silverstein's sidewalk ends and enter the thicker part of the jungle. While we had been walking past lime trees (that the locals called "limons"), mango trees, starfruit trees, breadfruit, tangled cornfields, and manioc plants, these give way for the thicker vine covered trees that soar above us. Festooned with vines, decorated with bromeliads and clinging orchids, it is very much like a steamy, two-hour hike through the glassed-in Palm Room of Longwood, the famous botanical gardens near Philadelphia (but with mud trying to suck your boots off.) Ashuco notices me slipping in the mud. Motioning us to stop a minute, he helpfully hacks down a sapling and fashions me a good walking stick (which I used the whole week.)

While we pause, Coriander remarks, "At least we didn't get our shoes muddy wearing these boots, but it's not doing much for keeping my feet dry. It's leaking in my right boot."

"Hey, you're doing better than me! Both of mine are soggy," I replied with a laugh, as we continue on our way.

Ashuco points at a tree with machete marks all over it, and mentions that it is for medicine.
"Dese is de Ficus. Ficus Insipida," said Ashuco, stating its Latin name. "Dese resin is used for de stomach. Parasites in de stomach."
He demonstrates by making a small cut in the bark and immediately a white, latex-like resin begins to ooze from it. Dabbing his finger in it, he shows us how it is thick and sticky.

Later, when I look it up, apparently it was so effective a remedy that pharmaceutical companies had chopped too many trees down (because more of the resin could be extracted that way) resulting in extirpation (localized extinctions) around the Amazon, thus causing a huge increase in stomach parasites in those areas. The short-sightedness of some people in the quest for immediate wealth is so frustrating! I treasure all the stewards of the land, like Ashuco, who carry the knowledge and use it in balance with the natural rhythms of the land.

Ashuco brings us to another tree and using his machete he takes scrapings from the inner bark. Squeezing the shavings in the palm of his hand, the juice dribbles along his down pointed thumb where he captures a small pool of liquid in his other palm.
"Try eet," he said, stretching out his cupped hand, dipping his forefinger in and dabbing it on his tongue. We mimicked him.
"It tastes... like bark," said Coriander dryly. But Ashuco goes on to espouse its many healing properties; cancer, ulcer of the stomach, etc.

I am struck with an "aha moment" on the concept of shamanic "medicine." For them, gathering up threads of power and weaving healing songs is no different than taking scrapings of bark from the natural world for medicine. It is there and exists, one needs only to gather it up.

Walking on, we come across an impressively large ficus tree, with fin-like roots spreading out from the base like organic flying-buttresses on this cathedral-like tree. Ashuco enthusiastically shows how to drum on the "fins" that are only a few inches thick; the sound echoing hollowly, the deep music of the trees joining in with the continual chorus of birdsong. He leads us into the steamy jungle to successively larger and larger ficus trees, describing how the trees provide homes for so many animals. He points out a hollow in a tree and peering into its depths we can see some tiny bats clinging to the inside of their dark wooden cave. Ashuco starts making a chirping, squealing noise, and two tamarind monkeys come to investigate. Ashuco laughingly explains he is making the call of a baby tamarind, but the tamarinds catch sight of him and warily stay high up in the tree canopy.

We had been working our way towards a giant ficus tree that had many lianas cascading down from it. Someone had cut some of the vines and built a little raised launchpad. Grinning like a little kid, Ashuco grabs a strong liana, climbs the launchpad, and gripping tightly to the vine, swings out about fifty feet (fifteen meters) and then back.
"I've got to try that!" exclaims Coriander, eagerly running over to the jungle swing! I film her gracefully swinging across the clearing under the huge jungle tree, like a modern day Jane, with a smile going from ear to ear.

By this point, it is now well past noon and the day is getting oppressively hot for me. I apologize that I don't think I can go any deeper into the jungle, so we start wending our way back. Ashuco's sharp eyes spy a hand-sized tarantula up in a palm tree and he points it out to us. We enjoy looking at it from a comfortable distance. During our walk, Ashuco has been pointing out various birds as they flit along above us: many brightly colored parakeets, some green hummingbirds, and a really large variety of woodpecker with a red crest, who rivals our pileated woodpeckers of North America.

We pass brilliant orange-yellow ginger flowers, which Ashuco explains is in the ginger family. Coriander teases me about my frequent stops to photograph butterflies and flowers, saying if I stop for every one we'll never get out of the jungle! Which is probably true considering how many lovely bromeliads we keep coming across and so many other flowers I have no name for.

I am fascinated when Ashuco points out a rubber tree. Someone had sliced it previously and there is a long, thin drip of gray rubber that runs down the trunk. Ashuco carefully uses his machete to pry the rubber off of the tree and hands us each a piece. Coriander playfully stretches it back and forth like a rubber band, then jokes, "Maybe I can patch your boots with it!"

The sweat is running freely over me as we return to the village, but finally I breathe a huge sigh of relief as the cool breezes off the Amazon river reach me. Once on board our boat, I dangle my hand over the side, soaking my hand in the cooler water, and splashing it over my forehead and cheeks. Noticing I had finished off my bottle of water, Coriander kindly offers me the last of hers.

Jungle swing

First thing upon our return to our hut, I peel off my sweat soaked clothes and hop into the shower, producing enough noises of pleasure at the cool water to get an embarrassed wail of, "Moooommm!" from Coriander in the bedroom. Laughing, I recall creating my pastel painting two years ago of the Goddess of the Desert. The inspiration came after a dangerously hot and parched hike in the Mohave desert. Feeling rather close to that at the moment, I think maybe I should create a Goddess of the Amazon as a matching artwork. I am so thankful for the blessed cool water.

Once I bring my body temperature down some, we go over to a late lunch of rice, and what seems like home fries but the potatoes are sweeter. Upon my remarking on it, Ashuco proudly states that there are 5,000 varieties of potatoes in the world and Peru grows 4,000 of them. Coriander is delighted with the steak strips, but in this heat, the thought of meat makes me feel nauseous. I'll stick with the cool and refreshing tomato and cucumber salad (and lots and lots of water!)

We are joined by another guest who is only staying for three days. Her name is Julie and she's from a cattle ranch in Nebraska. Apparently she can only handle the monotony of the cornhusker state for so long and then she gets wandering feet. Julie tells us about her past solo travels to India, Egypt, and Tibet, and now this trip has her in the Amazon working her way down to Antarctica. In this heat, my mind boggles at the thought of transitioning to the bitter cold temperatures of the Antarctic. "How can you pack for both climates?" Coriander exclaims, "You must have a ton of luggage!" Julie says she plans to purchase a parka and warm clothing once she gets to Antarctica. Coriander stays to chat with her but I have a bit of a headache and need to get a nap!

A short storm blew through, lowering the temperatures a smidgen, which I'm glad about but I awake with my headache much worse. And tonight is supposed to be our ayahuasca ceremony, I think with dismay! I had taken some ibuprofen before I fell asleep, but the medicine hasn't touched it. I decide to go over to the screened-in dining hall where there's a little more of a breeze. I am lying on the cushioned couch with my eyes closed as Ashuco walks through and Coriander explains I have a headache.

"Wait a meenute. Wait a meenute," he says, and off he goes outside. He comes back with some damp, deep-green leaves that he places on my forehead and I lay in the quiet for about a half hour.

Ashuco comes back inquiring about how I am doing. "It feels cool, which is nice," I say, "But the headache still hasn't gone away." He says he will get something else and off he goes into the jungle. Coming back, he holds in a bowl some green goop of a plant that he had mashed up. He gently applies this concoction to my forehead and puts another long leaf on top of it. The cooling plant mixture is soothing on its own, but after a bit, I can feel that the pain is starting to ease. I am concerned that the headache will interfere with the ayahuasca ceremony and mention this, but both Ashuco and the other guide, Homer reassure me that the ceremony will take care of the rest of my headache. I also remember reading a book on ayahuasca by my friend, Tommy Bailey and he had the same experience going into a ceremony. The ayahuasca cleared up his headache, so I'm trusting to that.

Jungle
Medicine

We are in darkness. I am in the middle in front of the Shaman with Coriander on one side and our fellow traveler, Julie, on the other. We are sitting on a thin cushion on the floor, arrayed in a line with our backs to the screen room wall. Next to each of us is our emergency bowl in case of vomiting which we know can be a side effect of ayahuasca. It is looked upon as your body purging past traumas, illness, and bad experiences. Ayahuasca's name means "vine of the soul."

The Shaman sits crosslegged on the floor in front of us, an older man with a face like a wrinkled brown walnut, who had been our weathered boatman by day. In the dim, shifting light, it seems that each time the light changes, he shows a different face of a thousand Amazon shamans before him, an unbroken line of teachers that spans many centuries.

He calls for illumination to set out his ritual space. First, a reused plastic burlap-type sack spread flat forms his work surface, several hand-rolled cigarettes, a narrow, clear plastic bottle filled with a dark liquid that must be the ayahuasca. Three little gourd cups are set out for us and one near him. Another smaller bottle with clear liquid, a dried bundle of what looks like narrow palm leaves forms his rattle, and the two gifts that I gave him (Native American tobacco and a creamy, white crystal point) are laid out carefully forming his "altar." The crystal looks so incongruous in this world of silt, sand and clay. I hope that it's a nice novelty to him, rather than a strange, out-of-place object in jungle medicine.

He speaks and another man translates his words, "This is a mixture of three plants: chacruna, ocoyage, and yage." The translator explains that the Shaman will now call the spirits. With that, the Shaman begins a low breathy whistle. Only stopping to light one of his cigarettes and blow smoke over his altar, the bottle of ayahuasca, and carefully into each of the tiny calabash cups laid out for us. He blows smoke over me. I flinch, expecting the gray choking scent of cigarettes, but instead a brown scent of burnt earth mixed in with tobacco washes over me. He hands the cigarette to Ashuco behind him and the translator explains to my surprise that Ashuco is his student. The Shaman starts shaking his palm leaf "rattle", the shush-shush of the rattle and his breathy whistle make it easy to relax into the ritual.

From outside, I hear a distinct call of an animal, "a deep descending, bubbling sequence: "PUP-pup-pup-pup-po." It is the call of the spectacled owl perched just outside our enclosure and it calls several more times, speaking to me, "I penetrate the darkest night and pierce through illusions. I am the Messenger between the worlds. I wing through the liminal spaces between this world and the next, traveling between the realms to bring Spirit's message to the Shaman. You know me now, and I am with you in your journey."

My attention is brought back to the Shaman as he indicates that I should put out my hands. He pours some of the clear liquid into my palm and the translator says we should rub it on our face and forearms. It tingles like 150 proof alcohol as I rub it on my forehead and cheeks. The Shaman carefully pours the ayahuasca into our gourd cups, pours one for himself and drinks it. When he hands us our cups, the translator explains to drink it all down.

I drink. It's not terribly unpleasant, rather astringent with an earthy taste like oak tannins. The Shaman sings his songs, timeless and mesmerizing. I zone out for a while, carried away on the singing. It is interrupted by a moment of extreme nausea, but it is quick and minimal, as I hadn't eaten dinner. At one point, I feel very, very hot, just overwhelmed with rushing heat. I remind myself that I had given birth and I can breathe through this and again I am carried away on the song.

The translator gently breaks into the reverie and explains that the Shaman will sing his fourth and final song. I feel a bit dismayed, since I had hoped for something more vivid; having heard of visions, images, and messages that had happened to others. I reassure myself that Mother Ayahuasca knows best and perhaps she is silently working at physically healing something within me. Soon the Shaman's song comes to an end.

I thank the Shaman, as I get wobbly to my feet. My balance is really off, so Ashuco takes my arm and makes sure I don't fall off the plank walkway and "stepping logs" in the dark. He gets Coriander and me safely back to our cabin. As I enter our room and get into bed, I realize that my headache is completely gone. The curtains swish and murmur in the cool breezes after the storm. The air, soft as a kiss, washes across me as I slip silently into a deep, refreshing sleep.

Ayahuasca Ritual

Friday: A Gentle Two-Hour Stroll Through the Jungle Behind Our Cabin - Butterflies - Piranha Fishing

I wake up with a glowing feeling after the ayahuasca ceremony. As I get out of bed, I feel a small touch of vertigo, but my mind is suffused with joy and contentment. The temperature is a little cooler than it has been, which makes me happy and I look forward to the day's adventures.

A week before we embarked for Peru I had found at the thrift store, a leather Indiana Jones hat that seemed fortuitous for the trip. I am friends with the artist, Anibal Zog from Brazil and he always wore such a hat, plus I had the example from the movies. I was trying to blend in to the culture of the Amazon. What I didn't know until I got there, that if you wanted to blend in you wore swim trunks, a battered American t-shirt, and a ball cap.

But it was shade, so with a big grin at Coriander, I don my Indiana Jones hat with the appropriate theme music, "dum de-dump DUM!" and we are off!

As we come out of our cabin, Ashuco flashes his golden-toothed grin.
"Vaminos!"
"Off we go," Coriander agreed.

He takes us on a long looping path around the back of our cabins. Passing a little bit of domesticated sugar cane and the tall manioc, we enter the deep overarching jungle. Ashuco had been explaining about the native tribes and how they make blowgun darts. "Dey use de poison from the poison arrow frog. Dese hit de monkey. De monkey go, 'Ay, what's dat?' Brush eet away, he think a fly and den he fall down." We stop a moment in a clearing while Ashuco steps a little distance away, off our narrow path to cut a hard part of a palm to whittle into a dart for us.

Coriander suddenly lets out a short shriek, "I'm not alone in my pants!" I look over at her and her hand is clutching a fold of material pulled away from her thigh.

"I think I killed it, but I'm afraid to let go!" she says in a strangled voice. We both start laughing at her predicament.

"Well, pull off your pants," I suggest. "I'm sure Ashuco has seen naked savages before."

"No! I'm not going to do that!" she says, with self-conscious indignation.

When Ashuco steps back to us, we explain the predicament. He very politely grabs the offending lump and gently works his other hand up her pants on the outside of her leg to remove the object. With a mischievous grin, he opens up his hand to display the mangled, bloody carcass of a large, crushed grasshopper and gets an expression of disgust from Coriander until we both break into giggles again.

Walking on the narrow path cut through the jungle, we keep coming across wonders. Ashuco points out webbing that stretches in a kind of tangled hammock shape over three feet (one meter.) Within the webbing are many small spiders scurrying around. Ashuco tells us that these are the "social spiders." Apparently they work together to capture prey that can be many times their size, or I suppose, first come, first served on smaller prey!

There are so many beautiful flowers and many more high above our heads in the tree canopy. I spy one that Ashuco tells me is an orchid, but it looks more like a red blossoming pinecone. Ashuco explains how many plants and animals have a symbiotic relationship, pointing out a narrow tree trunk.

"Dese tree trunk is hollow and makes a home for de ants. De ants protect de tree. Ees symbiosis. Dey work together," Ashuco said.

"Watch dese."

He starts tapping on the outside of this plain looking tree and, as if from nowhere, a thousand ants come swarming towards where he is tapping! Their tiny voices all chiming in at once, "What's going on?! What's up?! Is there danger?
We back up quickly, leaving the tree alone, and the ants begin to calm back down, "Nothing to worry about. False alarm. Back to work. It's just that tricky Ashuco!"

We come across a small make-shift bridge over a streamlet. Before we cross the logs, Ashuco excitedly points down into the mud at a four-toed footprint as large as his palm. "Dese is de jaguar! De jaguar footprint. You see?!" The thought that the print is relatively fresh and the jaguar must have passed some distance behind our camp in the night, is very exciting, but I can feel the hairs rise on the back of my neck. In all the native religions in this area, the jaguar always symbolizes a powerful shamanic force. I'm filled with awe thinking he had been silently walking nearby when we had been sitting in the Shaman's ceremony.

Ashuco's love of the jungle is very evident. With a swift scooping movement and a boyish grin, he opens his hand and shows us a baby bufona frog. A little bit further and he scoops up an adult version and points out how they perfectly blend into the brown, mottled leaves on the forest floor. Much to my delight, he catches a tiny little gecko. He passes it to me to hold and marvel at its fairy-like little feet and long delicate tail. It looks at me quizzically for a moment, then seems to make a decision, saying, "Gotta go!" and in a swift movement makes a dash off my hand. He would have fallen several feet, if I hadn't been quick enough to lower him down, so he landed in the soft leaves.

After two tries, Ashuco catches us the quick and elusive poison dart frog and Coriander snaps a couple of quick pictures before it makes a dash for freedom. As we travel along the path, we get a pretty good look at a much larger gecko on a palm trunk, but he taunts, "Can't catch me, I'm much too quick for you!"

We come across a cute little lean-to about four feet high, with palm branch "flooring," and a woven palm branch roof. Ashuco says later in the week, we can sleep in the tree-house, and on another night, we will be sleeping here. He bends down under the thatched roof and scootches in to sit down. Coriander and I both look a little dubious at him. Coriander climbs in and sits down next to him, to try it out, but she says, "I don't know... I love the idea of sleeping high in the treehouse, but I'm not so sure about on the ground." Ashuco reassures us that we will have a bed roll and mosquito netting, but then goes on to tell us about the lady who had an anaconda snuggle up next to her in the night. "He just like de warm."
Coriander looks at me with a "no-way-in-hell" look and I silently agree with her

despite Ashuco's reassurances. As we walk further, and discover more interesting insects, I think our resolve grew. The tree house sounded cool, but under the lean-to, with creepy crawlies... I don't think so!

Ashuco notices a mouse-size hole in the ground and starts "doodling" with a thin branch. He explains, "De ground tarantula theenk eet a little rat tail and eet might catch deener." As he is speaking, a hand-sized, hairy tarantula climbs out of its den looking for a meal, but it is just that tricky Ashuco! Coriander gets some photos from a comfortable distance, but we are happy to let it return to its little hideaway.

We find Ashuco puts Doctor Dolittle to shame with his knowledge of the language of the animals. Pursing his lips, Ashuco makes a high-pitched squeaking noise, causing a local monkey tribe to come furiously rushing over. They were leaping and swinging about in the tops of the trees, flinging themselves from branch to branch. Coriander and I both gasp as one of the marmosets misses the limb that it is aiming for and hurtles down fifty feet (fifteen meters) to the ground. Coriander anxiously asks Ashuco, "Is he dead? Did he kill himself? What did you do?!" There is a long enough pause that we are beginning to think it must be dead, but then we see it climbing (maybe a little shakily) back up a nearby tree.

The marmoset shakes his head as if to clear his thoughts and flicks his tail at us, "You tricked me again, Ashuco! I thought you were an invading group of monkeys! Oh, you got me mad!" We get a great look at his striped tail as it scampers back up and flicks his tail dismissively at Ashuco, who only laughs.

It feels like we are in a television nature special, as we come across a long parade of leaf cutter ants. I feel like I should be hearing the nature documentary narrated by David Attenborough, instead we have Ashuco in his heavy Peruvian accent telling us, "De leetle guide ant, he say go dese way, dat way, no, no, go to dese side! Dese side!" Ashuco points out the tiny guide ants that are riding on the cut leaves carried by the bigger worker ants, then he picks up the large worker ant and turns him in the opposite direction. First, it starts walking against the parade of other ants, then it wobbles around confusedly, and finally gets back on track walking with the rest of them, all carrying the fragments of green leaves back to their nest. Coriander asks, "What are they carrying the leaves for?" Thanks to the Disney nature specials of my childhood, I am able to answer her. "They are actually farmer ants. They take the leaves back to their nest and cultivate a fungus on the composting leaves that they then eat."

We see three huge, black centipedes about four inches long, looking like armor plated vehicles. I tell Coriander to take a photo with my hand near it.

"No one's going to be able to tell how big it is, without something in for perspective."

Ashuco points to a palm tree with long wicked-looking spikes all up and down the trunk, and identifies it as a chambira palm. He explains that the spikes protect the palm fruit from the jungle rat, but that natives will sometimes cut the tree open to extract the delicate, inner leaves that are forming inside because it is a good medicine to cure hepatitis and malaria.

Jungle Hut

When we get back to camp, we are joined over lunch by our adventurous American, Julie, who is traveling alone and two English fellows, Michael and Gregory, who had just come in. It makes for fun conversation. The English fellows are enthusiastically telling us about their adventures in Iquitos, eating the toasted grubs called "suri." Describing it as "salty" and "meat-like." Coriander expresses her disappointment, "I was hoping they were more like crispy potatoes chips." She still thinks she may give it a try when we pass back through Iquitos. The Brits also had an adventure on the way here when a fish jumped right into their boat and landed on Gregory's lap, flopping about. When their guide finally subdued it, Gregory was aghast to see it had very big teeth and was flopping about, as he described it, "dangerously near his nadgers."

At the other (much more subdued dinner table) are three Peruvian folks visiting. From their ages it looks like a mom, dad, and grown daughter. We guess they come from the city, since they seem fairly well dressed. Although they speak no English, it is amusing to see that their clothing has English words on it. The mom is dressed with a fancy necklace, diamond wedding ring, and a rhinestone decorated shirt that says "Baby" in elegant script.

Waiting to go piranha fishing, I am sitting in the shade in the little porch on our cabin. The sun has come out in the clearing in front of me and everything is so brilliantly vivid; the cerulean sky and the verdant jungle, shades of deep green, emerald, olive, lime, and jade. The breeze slides over my skin like silk. I am sitting on our little porch, watching the butterflies dance. Four pale yellow ones do a circle dance around each other, whirling like dervishes, a brown spotted butterfly alights near me for a second, two brilliant yellow ones flutter by, a large, pale green one catches my eye but is gone in a moment, and a few large dragonflies zip through. I feel like I'm caught in a gentle whirlwind of dancing petals, caught up in their silent singing. "Every moment is fleeting! Enjoy each moment and every passing breeze! Let your heart dance with us!" On and on they sang and danced in that timeless moment. I was startled back to reality when Ashuco called his familiar, "Vaminos!" to walk down to the boat.

Butterflies

How To Fish For Piranha:
Step 1: Get a bamboo pole and attach a line and barbed hook.
Step 2: Cut up meat scraps into 1/2 inch pieces and bait hook.
Step 3: Splash the water with the tip of your pole to attract piranha.
Step 4: Toss in the baited hook. When you feel a nibble pull up and replace the missing bait. Repeat.

No, it wasn't really that bad, but thinking about it afterwards, we probably traded an equivalent poundage of bait for poundage of fish.

All the piranhas we see are generally the size of your palm, shimmery silver with a splash of gold-red around their head. They are really quite pretty until you look close at their sharp teeth and jaws that take up about one fifth of their body.

Coriander excitedly hooks the first one, but it gets away before she can pull it back in. Then, one of the Peruvian family catches one. Their guide, Homer, takes it off the hook and shows us its large jaws and sharp teeth. Julie exclaims, "I can see where that would strip a cow in thirty seconds!" Coriander, with her eclectic homeschool knowledge corrects her, "They actually don't deserve their terrible reputation. That happened when Theodore Roosevelt was traveling through the Amazon. Some locals penned off a group of piranhas for several days. When Teddy Roosevelt came along, they tossed in a dead cow and of course the starving piranhas made short work of it, but it's actually pretty rare for them to kill anyone."

I catch a fish and Homer comes over to remove it from the hook. The shimmering piranha flashes in the sunlight and gnashes his teeth at me, "I'll take a bite out of you! You may be bigger, but I'll try to take you out!" I silently apologize to him but he adds belligerently, "What are you apologizing for?! I eat other fish all the time, now you'll eat me! But I'm not going out without a fight! Neither should you!" He flicks his tail contemptuously at me as he joins the other fish in the bottom of the boat.

Homer points out that we have three people from Peru and three of us from the U.S., so he declares it "Team Peru vs. Team U.S.!" (Although everybody cheers whenever anyone catches a fish.) Team Peru's mama figure wound up being the best at it and we promptly dub her the Champion, to which the Peruvians start mimicking the band Queen, singing their variation of "You are the Champion" in heavy Spanish accents. In the end, I think it was their 16 fish to our 14, but we toss back all but the 10 biggest, which we will eat for dinner.

We motor in our boat back to pick up our two English companions who had gone to visit Monkey Island, then navigating the junction of the tributary, we come to the point where we had seen many people swimming. Homer explains that locals use the mud to smear all over them because "it's medicinal." Coriander laughs, "I know! You guys keep saying *everything* in the jungle is medicinal!"

I have my bathing suit on, so I am delighted to get into the warm water. It is still refreshing after the hot, sunny day. I feel gratitude that we were able to spend most of the hot afternoon on the boat on the water, with a gentle breeze blowing up the Amazon.

Coriander rolls up her pant legs and wades in. She samples the medicinal mud, spreading it on her face and arms, but she quickly rinses off her hands, and grabs her camera to get a picture of our English boys who had slathered their entire bodies with the dark mud and were now making dramatic muscle man poses and fierce faces like Maori warriors.

I pick up a handful of the mud, looking thoughtfully at its deep umber color and the texture of the slippery clay that includes an underlying silky, firmness of silt. This earth that gently confines the boundless energy of the Amazon river, providing stability and structure, a place for us to stand and start out from. I smooth the mud over my arms and body, like a cool caress of Mother Earth. I let her medicine sink in as I look over the broad expanse of the mighty Amazon river, the lowering sun making spangles on the small waves. Over this broad expanse of water, the huge cumulous clouds move and shift, sailing slowly onward.

For a while, I lay back and float with my eyes closed, the sun forming dappled patterns against the inside of my eyelids. I feel myself supported by the element of life, an element that we are immersed in from the moment we first swim in the womb. I feel myself gently rocked with the small waves caused by wind and others moving around me. It reminds me that we must constantly be moving and learning, so as not to get stagnant.

I rise up from the water when Coriander calls excitedly, "Ma! Look! Look at the dolphins," my eyes following where she is pointing. The sun was just turning towards soft evening colors, and I can see the dolphins across the broad expanse of the river leaping high out of the water against the pink and violet sky. Their faint voices saying, "Take joy in this day! It will never come again! Join in the swimming. Join in this dance that is the cycle of life."

(And yes, we had the piranha for dinner, although Coriander's evaluation was that they were like Maryland crab, an awful lot of work for just a little meat.)

The sun starts to go down around 6 PM each night, at which point they run the generator for the lights. At seven, we eat dinner in the large screen room, and charge up our cameras or computer batteries at a side table with two power strips that they have set up, then we can retire to our cabins which have no light switches. Our cabin's single light bulb goes out around 9 PM when they shut the generator off. The generator is a good distance away because we can't hear it.

That evening we hear a frog voicing a great big "braaap!" out of our screened-in dining room rafters. Homer says that the saying is, "When the frog sings in the house, it means rain." Coriander laughs and says, "That's cheating! It's the rain forest. It's always going to rain at some point!"

I'm beginning to get used to hearing the potoo every night, "A forlorn series of whistled notes, the first, the longest descended to pitch, "Waooo, woo, woo, wooh-wuuh," according to the Birds of Peru book (which Coriander comically described as, "A huge, heavy book that you could kill a jaguar with.")

As I'm drifting off to sleep, I hear the underlying message of the nightly potoo, "I hunt the moth and mosquito and sing

love songs to the moon. All is well. All is
well. The night is so beautiful. Sleep
well."

Piranha fishing

Saturday: Morning Bird Walk - The Native Yagua Tribe - The Treehouse

Ashuco was excited to take us out at 6 AM in the morning to spot birds. To which Coriander gave her "no way in hell" look under lowered eyebrows and informed him that she didn't *do* mornings.

I get up at six, loving the cooler morning hours with a bit of a morning breeze. Ashuco leads us on a leisurely two hour walk in the area between the Amazon river and around the camp. We see so many birds, it's hard to keep track of all of them, and it's as if they are all talking at once!

We watch a small woodpecker, until a big woodpecker swoops in and takes over the spot, claiming, "My spot! My bugs!" Down by the water is a hunting osprey, waiting fairly patiently in the tree, wheedling, "Come out, come out little fishes!"

Wading in the marshes is the jacana bird that looks dark and nondescript except for his orange beak, then he takes to the air with a joyful cry, and the yellow wing feathers are revealed, making him a flash of color over the grasses. We see a huge, pheasant-like bird that Ashuco identifies as a hoatzin. It is dark with a messy tuft of feathers cresting its head. It perches on a leafless branch and then takes soaring flight over a marshy area revealing its russet under-feathers, soaring by with the message, "Enjoy the morn!"

A little green hummingbird flies down and perches on a cornstalk near us, so we can get a good look at him, "I'm beautiful, am I not? Can't stay! I'm off!"
Ashuco is excited to point out the rarer macaw as it flies overhead, a flash of yellow and blue. It shouts, "I am the pride of chiefs! The colors of royalty! Catch me if you can!"

There are flycatchers, seedeaters, tanagers, flocks of raucous parakeets, all prattling on about everything and nothing. Down by the banks of the Amazon we see two powerful and graceful roadside hawks, keeping their own silent council.

Ashuco assures me that we can borrow Homer's bird book and take a closer look at all the birds we are seeing. Ashuco amazes me with his encyclopedic knowledge of all the different birds, and I find it even more astounding to think he had probably learned all their names first in his native language, then in Spanish, and then in English (and some in Latin.) He can tell from the way the silhouette of the bird swoops against the sky, what variety it is, or tell me the name, just from a soft birdcall in the distance. He says he went to school for four or five years and then he "learned the jungle" from his grandfather. He has been a tour guide for about 25 years, yet still has the same joy of discovery as a young boy!

Morning Bird Walk

After breakfast, we take the boat down
to see the native Indian tribe, the Yaguas.
We pass a few fishermen out in long
shallow boats like ours, but without a
shaded roof in the middle. There are
usually two of them, flinging out their net,
rowing along, and then finally pulling it
back up again. One boat seems to be just
heading in the direction of Iquitos with
their little motor puttering away, a
temporary laundry line strung up to take
advantage of the breeze.

Our boat is full! We drop off the English
chaps in their "wellies" to go hike in the
jungle. (Coriander has decided that
"wellies" is a much better term than plain
old "boots" or "galoshes.") That leaves
nine of us: our three Peruvian tourists
with their guide, Julie with her guide, and
Coriander and myself with Ashuco. We
dock at one of the make-shift steps that
scale the steep banks of the Amazon. We
hike past a more modern settlement, in
that they seem to have a little bit of
electric line run and a bit more walls. In

one screened-in room we see a computer! But the huts are still all built with scrap wood, palm leaf roofs, and maybe a bit of tin.

Ashuco points out the flowering bush, the chacruna, one of the ingredients sometimes added to ayahuasca, with its white and light purple, waxy-looking flowers. I think he says the root is used for the tea.

Ashuco also shows us a plant that he says is in the ginger family. It has dark berries like large grapes that produce a magenta dye as he crushes one in his hands, then it slowly darkens to purple. To my surprise, we pass an abandoned jeep that is now used for storage and for the life of me, I can't figure out how they got it here! The sight of the jeep jars my awareness that we have seen no vehicles in any of the little towns along the Amazon. It had just become so natural to just walk or boat everywhere.

We get to a small circular clearing that is fenced in with benches all around and bedecked with the jungle crafts that the natives make. As we walk through the bamboo gate, we are greeted by the tribe, all the little children line up to shake our hands, the adults behind them nodding in greeting. Most of them are dressed in grass skirts. The women wear a wide grassy necklace that covers their breasts, as a concession to the more prudish visitors. I find out later that the Yagua people use aguaje fiber to make their grass skirts, which comes from the moriche palm. Another one of those amazing trees in the jungle which provides a super nutritious fruit, the leaves provide soft but tough fibers, the sap can be drunk or made into palm wine, and the tender shoots can be eaten as a vegetable.

The chief wears a crown of braided palms with macaw feathers sticking up, reminding me of the bright blue macaw that I saw flying overhead this morning.

According to Wikipedia, the origins of the name "Yagua" may have come from a word meaning "'blood' or 'the color of blood', which is a likely possibility due to the Yagua custom of painting their faces with achiote, the blood red seeds of the annatto plant." (Annatto is used as body paint, sunscreen, insect repellant, a spice, a paint pigment, and used as a natural food coloring in lots of modern day foods.)

We sit down on a bench while the chief does a short speech in their own language and Homer translates it in both English for us and then Spanish for the Peruvian family. The chief explains that his tribe is not native to this location, but had fled from the rubber barons (which at first, I thought he was saying "robber barons" but it's probably about the same.) The chief says they would have been killed but they relocated here and hid. He explains he wishes to share some of their traditions with us.

First, they anoint us with annatto jaguar "whiskers" painted on our cheeks. We watch as the natives gather to do a circle dance around a tree that is in the middle of the clearing. Each member of the tribe grabs a tourist partner to dance with. A little girl about five grabs my hand, but she only knows how to walk around the circle. Coriander has a slightly older girl who is more into the dance and they twirl around some, but it doesn't matter, we are all laughing and having a great time.

They start a second dance where all the men line up with their hands on the shoulders of the man in front of them and all the women line up the same way. Coriander jokes, "So this is where the conga line comes from!" I sit this one out since I am already overheated from the previous dance and the mid-day sun, but Coriander joins in. The natives chant along together, circling around the central tree. A short demonstration dance follows. Four young boys line up with a long, fringed palm frond that stretches over all their heads and they each toot on little one-note whistle while they dance around the tree. Coriander dubs this the "Anaconda Dance" since they resemble the long sinuous form of a snake.

Next is blowpipe target shooting. Their blowpipe is much longer than the ones they are selling. It is about four feet long, with darts made out of dried, hard palm whittled down (Homer explains they use large piranha teeth to cut it) with tufts of cottony-looking stuff like fletching, to form a seal to blow against. Carved balsa wood creates the mouthpiece. They set up a little effigy target with a tiny grass skirt and behind that is a back-catch of woven palm fronds. I volunteer to shoot first, but with my glasses all steamed up, I don't even notice the actual target and just shoot into the center of the back-catch. Coriander, knowing how good I was at target sports said to me later, "I wondered how you missed," after I explained I hadn't even seen the little target fellow and we had a good laugh over that.

We each get two tries to shoot and while we did it, they put the chief's woven crown with macaw feathers on our head. It makes for a great photo. Our travel companion, Julie, mutters it's way too touristy, but Coriander points out it would be like Germans performing their native dance in costume and that seems to mollify her some. But that starts them joking about the natives going back to their village, taking off their grass skirts and getting back into the standard Amazonian outfit of swim trunks, maybe a Coca-cola t-shirt and ball cap.

The Yagua chief explains in this new world, they also need money and invites us to negotiate for their crafts. I had already decided I wanted to get a blow gun for my husband, when the chief comes over and shows me his crafted blowpipe with decorative woven straw, a balsa "quiver" of small darts, and decorated with macaw feathers. Fortunately they are fine with accepting American money. I get Coriander a necklace with a piranha jaw (to remember all our fun at piranha fishing), and another fascinating necklace with a serrated fish bone for my son's girlfriend. One native girl uses gestures to indicate to Coriander she wants to trade a handmade bracelet for Coriander's bandana, but we had found how essential a bandana was for keeping the sweat out of our eyes and cooling off with river water, so Coriander sadly shakes her head no.

With our little treasures from the Amerindian tribe we retrace our steps back to the dock, but we have to wait a while for our boat. Some other residents of the Amazon are waiting for their "water bus" (which I understand runs once or twice a day.) Among them is a young girl who has a pet toucan. She carries him around some in the crook of her arm and then puts him on the ground to follow her. With his large colorful beak and blue feet, he presents a comical, clownish figure as he contentedly waddles along behind her. The young girl is happy to have us take pictures of her and her younger sister. I give them each a pack of gum that I had brought from the U.S. for friendship gifts.

We watch a parade of young boys lugging up boards from a boat that had apparently dropped the lumber off at the bottom of the cliff by the river. They carry them longways, up their backs and clutch them over their heads. The littlest boy, about seven, only carries one board up the steep mud steps and on to the village, the older boys carry as many as four at a time. No wonder they grow up to be strong and wiry like our jungle guides!

Another boy around twelve brings down a long stalk of sugar cane, skillfully using his machete to strip off all of the tougher outer cane, then he snaps off pieces for all the kids there. Coriander remarks that in the U.S., people get all uptight about letting a kid use a knife and here they don't think twice about young kids wielding a foot-and-a-half long machete on a daily basis!

The other guide had provided his group of Peruvian tourists with sugar cane, so Coriander hollers over to where Ashuco is sitting, "Ashuco," she says in a mock teasing tone, "I'm getting jealous. How come they get sugar cane and we don't." He laughs, "You want sugar cane, okay!" He trots off to get a cane and a machete and serves us all some. It is fun to suck out the sweet juice and then spit out the fibrous bits that are left. We entertain ourselves watching the ants busily carrying off the sweet pieces on the ground.

Finally our pecamari shows up and motors us back to camp. Lunch is the usual rice, but with melt-in-your mouth tiger catfish in a mildly spiced sauce, the ever present tomato and cucumber slices, and I try a piece of manioc which I find a rather dull, cold, potato-like food. After lunch, Julie bids us farewell and leaves to make her way by cargo boat down to Antartica.

We are joined by a troop of six fellows from Poland, but they don't seem very sociable. In the afternoon, we all go off in the boat. The Polish fellows are dropped off to hike in the jungle, the English boys, Gregory and Michael are off to do piranha fishing and we get dropped off to go to the "treehouse" for the night. I have always loved climbing trees and looking out over the view below, and I find this a very exciting prospect to be sleeping high in the tree canopy of the jungle!

The Yagua

Saturday night to Sunday morning: The Treehouse

We walk across the largest plain that we've seen here, eventually passing the usual corn fields and tall manioc plants that surround a village. We're each carrying two plastic grocery bags stuffed full of bedding, mosquito netting, and food supplies. Coriander declares that the "Rule of the Jungle" means the person with the machete gets to go first, so Ashuco and his machete lead the way.

As we're walking, we start to hear the bone-deep beat of Dubstep music. Coriander and I both look at each other with puzzled faces, as if to say, "Are we really hearing that?!" and we laugh at the incongruity of electronica music in the jungle. The sense of unreality increases as we approach the little community of palm-thatched huts.

Our path emerges out past an open windowed hut built of the usual rough-cut lumber. Long-legged chickens stalk purposefully under the stilts supporting the house into the dusty shade of the residence. A rectangular mowed grass field opens before us surrounded by rough-cut lumber houses, all up on stilts. Chickens are running all around, under the houses and through the field, as modern dubstep is blasting out over the whole village. A few groups of kids play soccer at the ends of the large field, while most folks just sit on the floor of their porch, or lean on their elbows and look out open windows. A few hammocks are slung in the shade under the houses and they are full of women; one woman lazily nursing her toddler. Standing there on the sidewalk that encloses the field, we are an object of mild curiosity.

Ashuco stops at one of the houses, chats with them there in Spanish and eventually brings out a large ledger with lists of signatures that he asks us to sign. I guess it was to show that we were going into the jungle and to let them eventually track us down if we didn't come back. He disappears back into the house for a while and Coriander and I stand there still trying to take in all the strange contradictions; one toddler pushing the other on a plastic toy car in this land of no cars... the encircling cement sidewalk in this land of mud and wood... and the contrast of the primitive open-air houses with modern Dubstep reverberating through the entire village...

Apparently Ashuco arranged for two people to carry our bed rolls, mosquito netting, and food supplies, and once we get walking, they follow along at a distance behind us. We are also followed by a scrawny dog Coriander names Lulu Belle. As the Dubstep fades behind us, we follow Ashuco to the inevitable end of the sidewalk, and it turns off into a broad, cleared track, wider than any we had traveled before, about the width of a car. I don't know where it led or why it was so well traveled because eventually we turned off it onto the more usual footpath through the forest, but before we do, we keep stopping to observe more jungle wonders. I spy a cluster of multi-colored beetles, spotted in red, orange, blue, and yellow, even their legs are striped red and blue! They look just like squash bugs, but they must have been the psychedelic hippie cousins that moved to the jungle. Ashuco points out a large brown owl moth clinging to a withered leaf. It blends in almost perfectly, despite the eye-like circular markings on the wings, designed to scare off any predators who did manage to spot it.

"What do you think?" Coriander asks me as we trudge along. "Are we the Lost Boys or Swiss Family Robinson?" I think of the treehouse ahead.
"I think we're the Lost Boys from Neverland." I say. "They had lots more fun. The Swiss Family Robinson had a lot more work."

"Okay!" she happily agrees, "We're the Lost Boys!"

As we follow the narrow path through the jungle, a light drizzle begins to fall. "Ashuco," I tease, "You said there wasn't going to be a shower at this camp!" But I certainly wasn't complaining; the gentle rainfall feels nice after our exertion in the steamy heat. We finally arrive at a large screened-in room up on stilts, which is a distant part of the Maniti camp and a stopping place before continuing to the treehouse. As the evening starts to gather, Coriander and I hide in there from the oncoming mosquitos. We flop down on the pile of thin mattresses that apparently stay here. I clean off my glasses, which have gotten all steamed up again.

Ashuco, immune to the heat, the exertion, the light rain, and any mosquitos, starts to prepare our dinner under a small, palm thatched lean-to. It has been used many times for this purpose and there is a gracefully woven sack made of palm fronds containing re-used plastic bottles that are supposed to hold supplies. However, Ashuco discovers that the supply of matches are gone. He hollers over to us, "I be back een forty meenute!" and off he trots back to the village leaving us alone in the slowly darkening jungle. Lulu Belle abandons us in apparent disgust at our ineptness, and follows Ashuco back to the village.

Coriander looks at me, "Forty minutes? Do you think he can do that whole walk, to the village and back in forty minutes?! That just took us at least an hour!" I shrug and lay back down on the pile of cushions, but soon Coriander starts pulling out the thin mattresses from the folded pile behind me.

"What are you doing?" I ask bewildered. "I'm going to build a pillow fort... to protect me from the jaguars and mosquitos," she explains.

"It's not going to protect you from the mosquitos." I say, mocking an ominous tone. "Nothing can protect you from the jungle mosquitos. I think we've used up most of our DEET and it doesn't seem to help."

"Well," she adds mischievously, "I only have to hide from the mosquitos long enough for them to find you first!"

I laugh as she proceeds to unfold the thin mattresses, prop a stick diagonally in the corner to support her "roof" and drape the mattresses all around her, with two to sit on.

I leave the safety of the screened-in room to take a look at the nearby waterway and rowboat that we can see from the screen hut. It is very picturesque with bamboo and palms emerging from the water and the green pads of waterlilies and other vegetation floating all around. The term "swamp lettuce" comes to mind, but I don't know if that is a correct identification or not. I also take the opportunity of privacy to avail myself of a tree, which is the only bathroom facilities that we are going to see. (I must say, the finned roots of the ficus tree provides a convenient and private jungle bathroom stall.) I get a few photos before the mosquitos catch on that I am there and I have to retreat to the screened-in hut.

True to his word, Ashuco traverses the whole distance in an amazingly short amount of time and is back as tireless as ever (making me start to think that there really is something to that poison frog ceremony!) He looks puzzled at the conglomeration of thin mattresses in the corner, but Coriander playfully explains her cushy fort was to keep away the mosquitos and jaguars, and he joins in laughing at her whimsy.

We join him for a short period of time outside the protection of the screen room, watching as he uses his machete to expertly slice thin green bamboo stalks to form our grill, and piles dry wood underneath for the fire. Ashuco points

out a humungous frog, brown and green,
and bigger than both my hands clutched
together. Coriander is fascinated.
He teases Coriander, "We have frog leg
for deener. Yes?"
"No!" cries Coriander, who has already
bonded with the frog.
"Is good. Frog leg, good," his eyes
twinkle mischievously.
"No," I say laughing, "I think we'll stick
with the chicken you brought."
Soon the jungle is full of the delicious
scent of marinated chicken sizzling away
as the night seeps in.
"What kind of frog was that, Ashuco?"
"Eet's a big frog and a big name,
Leptodactylus pentadactylus."
"Ah, that's great," Coriander squeals, "I'll
have to learn that, Leptodactylus
pentadactylus," she repeats.
"Eet is called a smoky jungle frog."
"No, I like Leptodactylus pentadactylus,"
said Coriander happily, filing that away in
her memory.

As the whine of multitudes of mosquitos start to make us look like we are having a seizure trying to swat them away, we retreat back into the screen room. Ashuco, apparently totally immune to the insects brings in "jungle plates" as he calls them. Large, glossy, oval leaves that he identifies as maranta leaves, as he carries our grilled chicken and a previously boiled potato in on them. Fortunately, he gives me a rather large piece of chicken, so I save half of it for the next day, and half of the potato, knowing that breakfast consists of hard-boiled eggs that I'm not fond of.

We eat and watch as the fireflies come out, not blinking once or twice like we are used to, but communicating like little intermittent strobe lights flickering in the darkness. Coriander takes down her fort and selects the three cushiest mattresses for us to bring to the treehouse. Ashuco bundles a few of them up into a tight roll. We gather up our slightly lighter bags and step back out into the darkness. We walk

the short distance to the row boat and by the light of Ashuco's flashlight, carefully get ourselves and our bundles on board. Ashuco pushes us out into the partially submerged palms and bamboo, following a slightly cleared path through the aquatic vegetation, turning on his headlamp now and again to navigate where we are going. Coriander says in a hushed voice full of wonder, "There something glowing in the water! Ashuco, what's glowing?!"
"Eets de dragonfly larva."
We watch in awe, having a hushed conversation as to whether it is absorbing the light from Ashuco's headlamp and glowing from that, or if it is generating its own bioluminescence. We finally came to the conclusion that it seems like it is bioluminescent on its own.

Glowing dragonfly larva floating all around our canoe, swirling with every paddle stroke in the night, and all around our heads are the fireflies randomly strobing, with a few hazy stars above, and the occasional flicker of distant lightning…

truly we were the Lost Boys, in a canoe stolen from Captain Hook, piloted by our Indian brave flying through the starry night!

The treehouse is about fifty feet tall, with three platforms as we ascend. It looks rather like the fire-towers that they have in the PA woods, only not made out of metal but slapped together out of boards and narrow tree trunks. The stairs are uneven and steep, and tough for me to climb at the end of a very long day, but Ashuco quickly sets up our mosquito nets, rectangles of fine mesh tied to the platform railings to form a safe "box" over our thin mattresses. Coriander gets the very top, but that leaves Ashuco sharing my net on the next level down. I watch the flickering lightning above the tree line, feeling rather awkward lying next to him. Despite being in sweaty hot clothes I keep them on and finally fall asleep to the sound of a heavy rain starting.

Row boat to the Treehouse

Sunday: Waking in the Treehouse - Exploring Around the Island - Swimming With Dolphins - Night Walk

I wake early and the view is spectacular from the top of our treehouse. I look down onto a tree-filled watery expanse stretching out under a gray and pink pearly sky. A movement in the tree canopy catches my eye, and I watch as three large hoatzin birds stretch and climb about the upper branches nibbling on damp leaves. "It's a lazy, hazy day," they say, indolently stretching their wings. I can just see their tufted feathers on the top of their head, and their lovely cream and russet chests set off by their dark wings. "Look at our beautiful domain." They spread their wings to show me, then launch themselves heavily from the tops of the trees out over the tree canopy. Gliding over the fringed tops of palms, they remind me of pterosaurs gliding over some Jurassic jungle.

The rain has slowed to a gentle drip from the trees, but it doesn't cool off the steamy morning. Ashuco notices I am awake and calls my attention to the call of a pygmy owl; a high-pitched, repetitive sound, like "pweep, pweep, pweep, pweep..."

"This is my territory!" he cries from a nearby tree.

He is only about 6 inches high/17 cm, but the sound carries far out over the swamp below. Then our attention is caught by the flash of a large kingfisher swooping over the water below, looking for his breakfast of fish.

I reapply my bug repellant lotion, crawl out of our safe netting, and go up to check on how Coriander has fared on the level above us. She is still huddling in her mosquito netting.

"I'm not coming out," she says. "They're just waiting for me. I could hear them all night buzzing around saying, 'You've got to come out sometime!'"

"C'mon out," I laugh. "It's better in the morning, plus I've got bug repellant and you've got to see the view!"
I persuade her to emerge from the netting and she joins me looking out over the railing. I point out our watery path through the swamp, the majestic blue kingfisher, and the pheasant-sized hoatzin birds. The tree tops are thick below us. It was so worth every bit of effort getting out here!

We move down to the landing below us where Ashuco has packed up our netting and is starting to roll up our thin mattresses.
"Hey!" Coriander says indignantly.
"How'd you get two mattresses?" she asks me accusingly. "No fair."
"Oh, well," I say smugly, "I guess Ashuco likes me more."
"Fine," she teases Ashuco, "Playing favorites, I see!"
He just flashes his gold toothed grin.

Coriander says to Ashuco accusingly, "I thought you were going to sleep down on the first level, so I had two levels of protection from the jaguars."

"Oh! That's why the steps are uneven!" I say in mock discovery. "It was to trip up the jaguars."

"Right," she says dryly, "Because jaguars certainly couldn't leap up steps."

We descend along the uneven steps, leaving our bundles of bedding in the dry spot under the treehouse. I grab my walking stick, and Ashuco leads us out with a happy, "Vaminos!"

The Treehouse

We wind up hiking a loop around our swampy "island" learning about all the plants. Ashuco points out chinchona bark and explains that it is good against malaria. We come across large "cannon ball fruit," a dark, hard-husked fruit which looks exactly like its name. There are great looping vines, huge empty snail shells as big as my fist (the occupants apparently being eaten by other jungle denizens), but we don't see any caiman even though Ashuco makes a deep grunting noise to call them in.
"You can speak alligator?!" says Coriander in awe. "I didn't even know alligators made a sound."

As we walk along, the air becomes thick with the scent of jasmine and I see fallen flowers scattered all over the ground. I point them out to Coriander and explain that it is the same jasmine that flavors her favorite tea. Ashuco delights in showing us more of the "medicine" of the jungle. He cuts a chunk of "iron wood" and shows it to us.

"For de rheumatism," he says. "Make de tea. Smell eet."

I do, and it smells pleasantly spicy. I don't think it's the same tree that I know as "iron wood" or "muscle wood" that grows in the Pennsylvania woods. I tuck the chunk of wood in my tummy pack to bring back home. He also cuts a small slice of wood off a different tree and hands it to me, "Dese is rosewood." It does have a lovely pink hue and I tuck that away too.

Ashuco picks up an avocado sized "monkey fruit" from the forest floor and hacks it open with one swipe of the machete. Inside are several white grubs that Ashuco tells Coriander are breakfast. "I haven't had enough sleep to be that adventurous," she says. "I need to have enough sleep or enough coffee in my system to tackle adventures."

"Eets good. Coconut flavored," he assures us, as he happily munches a grub down, but he tosses "breakfast" away with a chuckle when we both vehemently shake our heads no.

Our loop takes us back almost to where we started, although Ashuco has to hack away some vines with his machete. We have to cross a log to get over a waterway covered in tiny green leaves. I am feeling grateful again for my trusty walking stick. There seems to be a lot more vines here on our island in the swamp and they are fascinating to photograph (and to climb!)

I pick up a big, round cannonball fruit and send it arching through the air. "Incoming!" I holler, as it plops down to land beside Coriander. I am teasing her for protesting getting her picture taken with one of the cannonball fruit earlier in front of the tree, "because" she said, "one's going to land on my head." I find out later that the Cannon Ball tree is amazingly useful: its antibiotic properties are used to cure colds, the antifungal leaves can cure skin infections, the inside of the fruit is antiseptic and is used on wounds, and the young leaves have analgesic qualities that help against toothaches. As Ashuco says, "Ees medicinal!"

We gather up our bedding and go back to the canoe. Ashuco points out a large pile of scat pellets near the waterway, each about the size of an adult thumb.
"Ees capybara sheet. Ees a big rat. A jungle rat."
Coriander quips, "That looks like it would be a lot bigger than the bamboo rat! I'm just glad I can't look up a picture of a capybara is right now!"

After we are in the canoe, Ashuco points out some capybara prints and a large wallow of the world's largest species of rodent. To which Coriander comments dryly, "I didn't know R.O.U.S's were really a thing, but... they're a thing."
She adds, "I already was feeling like we were the Princess Bride in the Fire Swamp back when Ashuco was hacking away the vines with his machete."

"Now we know the secrets of the Fire Swamp, we can live there quite happily," I say with a grin, as I quote back at her from the movie, "Along with the Rodents Of Unusual Size."
Ashuco laughs right along. I doubt he has ever seen "The Princess Bride," the movie we are quoting from, but Coriander's expression is comical enough.

The canoe ride back isn't as quite as magical as in the night, but it's still very beautiful as we are able to see the pink morning glories twining in the tops of the elephant ear palms. I confirm with Ashuco that it is water lettuce that thickly covers our waterway, parting as we canoe through it, and slowly drifting back in our wake. It is a gentle ride through the water and we don't talk much. The muffling influence of the gray day, and the trees rising above us like a cathedral, inspire a reverential silence. The soft, "plish" of the paddle propels us through the water, the occasional whir of a busy dragonfly, the constant lilting birdsong provides our background music, and fills me with peace. I feel like the ayahuasca ritual and sleeping in the jungle has tuned me in to more of its rhythm: the continuing rise and fall of the Amazon river, like the breathing of a great sleeping beast. The flitting of the human creatures over its surface has no more lingering effect than the flickering mayfly, compared to the greatness of Pachamama, the Earth Mother.

Too soon our gentle boat ride is over. Ashuco ties up the boat and helps us out onto the shore. We carry the bedding back to the large screen room. Ashuco asks us if we are hungry as he lays out some fresh picked "jungle plates." Coriander says, "I'm always hungry," as he lays out our breakfast: hard boiled eggs, cold potatoes, and the left-over chicken from the night before, which has attracted some tiny ants. I can tell I am getting used to the jungle, nonchalantly shaking them off, despite Coriander assuring me that it was "just extra protein." Ashuco teases her back for passing on the "extra protein" grubs this morning.

We pack up our slightly lighter bags and Coriander cleverly uses a stick to balance the two grocery bags on either end across her shoulders like a yoke. We trot back to the village, stopping long enough to photograph another large owl moth, and watch some lively squirrel monkeys. Further along the path, Ashuco's sharp eyes pick out a sloth moving slowly in the tree above us. We pause and watch him for a while. He seems to be a little more raggedy than the one we had seen at Monkey Island, but he might just be having a "bad hair day" because of the rain last night.

We walk through the village, and out to where the pecamari will pick us up on the Amazon river. Coriander gives us a mock-morning radio announcement, "Due to last night's rain, the morning commute will be slippery, with a slight chance of falling on your ass."

"Yes, there's a lot of mud," I agree.

"I know!" says Coriander, "I had promised my friend to bring back a rock from the Amazon. I thought I'd pick her up a river rock, but there's no rocks! It's all just mud and silt."

We both laugh over the absurdity of it.

"Yeah!" I agree, "Makes it kind of hard to do. Maybe you can bring her back some Amazonian mud… 'eets medicinal.'"

Our shaman/boatman picks us up. It is a peaceful ride back. Along the way, Coriander and I spot a group of animals grazing along the riverbank that look like goats from a distance. Ashuco is in the back of the boat motoring, and in the loud noise we can't get his attention to be able to point them out and ask him what they are. Later at dinner, when we are describing them to Ashuco I mention that I thought maybe they were goats or deer. He suggests armadillo. Coriander replies in an indignant fashion, "Now that makes me question everything you've told us all week! No wonder I have trust issues!"

"Maybe eet's a sheep?" he queries.

"Suuure... sheep or armadillo," Coriander says mocking skepticism, which gets us all laughing.

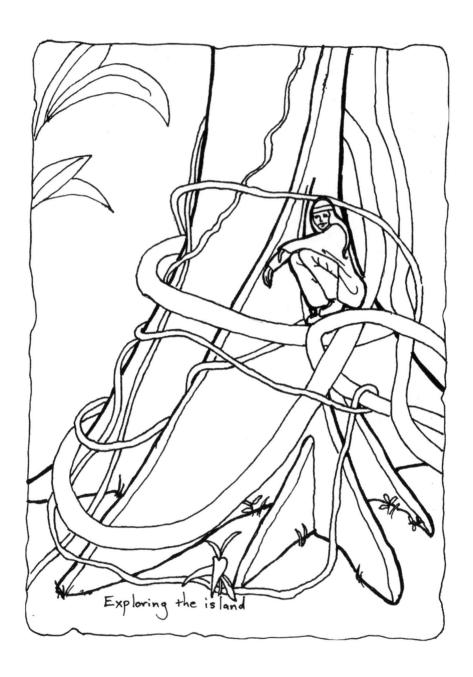

Exploring the island

Ashuco takes his leaf shaped paddle and stabs it deep into the sandy clay, then ties our canoe up to this make-shift pier. It's astonishing to see him standing knee deep when we are out at least a hundred feet (thirty meters) from the shore. He stabilizes the canoe, and I hop out into the brown and bath-water warm Amazon. Coriander follows with the stipulation that she's not going swimming. Holding her head high, she states imperiously that she's a long-legged wading bird and doesn't want to get her feathers wet. I'm enjoying the refreshing water and the slightly overcast sky. The clouds are in three different layers, like an illustration in a science book showing the difference between cirrus, cumulus, and cirrostratus.

We hear the puff of a dolphin exhaling. He sounds exasperated, "Clumsy creatures. Why do you stay on land?" but he doesn't wait for a reply and swims swiftly off. We spot several others out in deeper water. Every now and then we get treated to glimpses of the impressive, three-meter-long pink dolphin, its bright pink tail flipping out of the water. Ashuco points at them, "Look! Look!" as excited as a boy seeing them for the first time.

I recalled hearing tales of how the pink dolphins were actually people that had converted to this aquatic form. This belief on the Amazon is strong enough to keep these beautiful animals safe from hunting. Looking at their pale pink backs sliding through the water, I yearn to swim over closer and join them in their aquatic dance, later to slide down deep into their magical underwater cities.

Ashuco points at a gray dolphin that just joined them.
"Ees de juvenile," he says, his face crinkled in a grin.
Soon one comes up about twenty feet from us. We scan the slightly choppy water looking for the flick of a tail or arch of a back. At one point, we can see a gray dolphin playing with a floating stick, poking at it and even tossing it playfully.

Our patience is really rewarded when one pops up only ten feet away from us! It laughs at our surprise and dives gleefully back into the river. After that, they seem to be only out in deep water, so we just swim around in the shallows for a bit. It's so delightful to have no mosquitos buzzing about our heads and a delicious temperature after some brutally hot days. As we get back into the canoe, Coriander points out a tiny leak in the side of the boat. Ashuco grabs a handful of mud and uses it as a patch, causing Coriander to quip, "We're patching our canoe with mud... what could go wrong?" Ashuco just laughs at her. He had no problem paddling us safely back to camp arriving at the dock with the canoe only a little damper than when we left.

Dinner is the usual rice, a breaded fish, broccoli, plantain chips with a spicy relish/ pickle that was yummy on the chips, and fresh sliced pineapple for dessert. We miss our English boys, since with their appetites, we didn't have to worry about any leftovers from dinner going to waste, but I guess they had left before we got back from the treehouse. The fellows from Poland seem to have gone too. We are joined by two ladies from England who are adventuring together, and a lady from Korea who had been working at a job in Peru for the past year. Her job is done, so she is taking a quick week to see the sights before she returns to her home country. She is going to be leaving the same morning we are but has to catch an earlier flight. Talking and joking with the other ladies we come up with the t-shirt idea of "Life is better after DEET."

Swimming with Dolphins

Coriander hadn't wanted to do the night walk, so I left her chatting with our fellow travelers, and Ashuco and I head out on our boardwalk toward the river. Right at the beginning of our walk, we spy two big, gorgeous moths, one of which takes a shine to me and travels with me for a bit, clinging to my pants before fluttering off. We see several frogs, one that is as huge as my two fists put together, and a fascinating little one that is a pale milky brown, but glistening and almost transparent, as if it were made of gelatin and creamy coffee. I wish I can take a photo of it, but we are doing our walk by flashlight and in the low light and trying to swat away mosquitoes, I just don't have enough hands to take a picture.

When we come out from the canopy of the jungle, the skies open up above the Amazon river, I see more hazy stars and can pick out the group of the Pleiades. Orion seems to be lying awkwardly on his side. The fireflies are magical. They festoon the trees with their tiny strobe lights. There are also several thousand mosquitos, despite the gentle breeze off the Amazon river (causing me to think that perhaps Coriander had made the better decision.) I am dreadfully jealous, as Ashuco seems to be annoyingly impervious to them. When Ashuco aims his headlamp upward, we can catch the black flicker of a few overworked bats and I silently cheer them on. We are looking for owls along the river bank, but I finally have to give up under the onslaught of my flock of mosquitos. We start to head back and just as we approach camp we hear the trill of a screech owl. Ashuco locates him with his headlamp, a cute little thing high on a branch. He looks at me accusingly, "What are you still doing out? You're scaring off my meal!" I nod goodnight to him. Satisfied with the evening's animal observations, I happily depart towards my cabin. I blissfully cool off under my third shower of the day. Although as Coriander had joked earlier, "A shower in the steamy jungle seems kind of pointless."

As I'm lying there falling asleep, Coriander gets me giggling again with a sleepy comment, "Either there's a mosquito in here or I've developed tinnitus."

Night Bird Watching

Monday: The Search for Iguanas - More Dolphins

After breakfast we meet up with Ashuco. Coriander happily calls out, "Vaminos!" as we hop up on our plank path to follow it out to the boat. On the way Ashuco excitedly points out three yellow-tufted woodpeckers, as well as a yellow-headed caracara hawk. I am filled with awe at the diversity of life in the jungle!

We motor down the river. Another tour guide amuses us by taking a coconut palm leaf and doing "jungle origami"; folding and plaiting and cutting the leaf to form an adorable green grasshopper. Coriander likes this much more than the wild one that had climbed in her pants and keeps it as a treasured souvenir.

At last we come to another steep plank "staircase" up a twenty-feet-tall muddy cliffside. (How they tell one from the other, I'm not sure, but then again, I know where I am in the Pennsylvania woods by the curve of the road and shapes of the trees, so I suppose it's not that different.)

The day has warmed up swiftly under the bright, clear sky. We walk along between tangled cornfields and palms. Spotting some parakeets flitting about near a termite enclave in a tree (it looks a lot like a black, large, hornets' nest but wrapped around the tree trunk.) Ashuco explains how it's a symbiotic relationship between them. He points out a bird-sized hole in the bottom of the termite nest and explains that the parakeets live inside the termite nest. The female parakeet is welcome with the extra food she brings for her babies and their excrement provides food for the termites and the termites protect the nest. To illustrate, he taps on the nest and immediately the termites swarm out. Their tiny voices overlapping and belligerent, "Hey! You want a piece of me?! Who's that?! I will cut you!" They look around and begin to settle back down, as they pass the word,

"False alarm. Nothing to see here. It's just that tricky Ashuco."

We move on to a small grove of trees and spy a few pygmy marmosets, about the size of a squirrel. Two seem to be affectionately grooming each other high in the tree. I notice some wrinkly, green pods hanging from the trunk and branches and ask Ashuco about them. He confirms my suspicion that they are cacao pods (which I recognized from visiting the Hershey chocolate factory in the past.) I always loved the very appropriate Latin name for them, "theobroma" meaning "food of the gods."

It has gotten brutally hot and Coriander is teasing me about finding the shady spots the most fascinating. Also, as I move quickly from one shady spot, across a field to another shady spot, she says, "That's the first time I've seen you move faster than Ashuco!" We see a brilliant green hummingbird zoom close by, and

Ashuco points out a silver tanager, but we still haven't spotted an iguana.

Coriander is joking with Ashuco. He tells her that iguanas don't make any sounds, consequently, he can't call them like he has been doing with everything else.
She exclaims incredulously, "I think that's the only animal language you can't speak! I guess I'll just have to lure them in. I'll have to sing an iguana song," which she makes up on the spot:
"Iggy, iggy, iggy iguanaaaa.
You want to see me,
You know you wannaaaa.
My scales are green,
My tail is longaaaaa,
Iggy, iggy, iggy iguana!"

Switching to a rap beat, she sings,
"If you want to find me, then the jungle is the spot!
I like my forests, and I like them hot!
Iggy, iggy iguanaaaaaa!"

We have to cross a bridge made of two logs and Coriander comments encouragingly to me that I am getting good at crossing rickety bridges. Ashuco corrects her and says, "Dere not rickety bridges... dere Peruvian bridges!"

When we still can't find any iguanas, Coriander quips, "I guess I shouldn't have worn my anti-iguana-perspiration today. I just didn't think about it, you know?!" I think we are getting a little punchy from the heat because we are getting the giggles over everything. Coriander idly picks up a huge leaf and makes faces while pretending to be devoured by it.

I think Ashuco is feeling like he failed us by not finding any iguanas, but Coriander reassures him, "No, it's been great! We saw that hummingbird, some pygmy marmosets, I've come up with my first hit music song... Really! It's been great!"

Fortunately, we don't have to back track because the boat has moved around and is waiting for us at the end of the trail. I'm glad we are climbing down because it is a really tall cliff, about 40 feet, just steep steps cut into the clay, and zig-zagging down. The breeze on the river helps revive me with evaporative cooling. In the boat, I take off my hiking sneakers. Once we get back, I just walk barefoot back to camp for lunch. I have to hop over a spot on our log path where a swarm of army ants are crossing in a parade. I am feeling like each day in the jungle we are getting more and more used to it. Today is above average temperatures, but generally, with the average temperatures in this area around 90 degrees/ 32 Celsius, I think if I spend much longer here, I'll wind up wearing a grass skirt and going barefoot all the time!

Peruvian bridges

The sun is out and it is blistering hot. We put on our bathing suits, slather up with sunscreen, and walk barefoot down to the canoe with Ashuco. He sits up front on the seat and paddles, while we sit down lower on some boards that are placed in the bottom of the small canoe.

While Ashuco paddles downstream, I lazily trail my hands in the warm water on either side of the canoe. This wooden canoe is made with about six, bent, wide boards. The nails are hammered in from the outside and the sharp ends bent down inside the boat. The seams are sealed with some sort of tar and there is a slow leak in the bottom of the boat that prompts the occasional bailing with half a milk jug as a scoop. A few tenacious little grasses have taken root in the seams and add their bright cheery green to the weathered gray of the boards. Ashuco absentmindedly plucks at them as he scans the Amazon river for signs of dolphins.

We get to our nice shallow strand that we had used the other day and Ashuco anchors us again using the paddle sunk in the mud as a temporary mooring. Coriander is out in a flash into the refreshing water, since this little canoe doesn't have the shady palm leaf awning like the bigger boats. It does feel delicious after the heat of the sun.

Where it is shallow, we get down into the water and propel ourselves with our arms, like walking catfish, our legs trailing along behind us. It is still astounding to be out several hundred feet from shore and kneeling to keep most of our body submerged. For three hours we enjoy moving around in the water and looking for signs of dolphins. The most exciting bit is when the huge pink dolphins are about forty feet away. We can see their arching pink backs and fins and see them spray water from their blowholes.

"It's fun! Such fun," they call. "You are so silly to live on land!" they laugh. One blows a raspberry at us, making us dissolve into laughter.

The brilliant blue sky is accumulating huge fluffy cumulous clouds, one of which develops an iridescent shimmer of a rainbow cascading down the cloud. Later, we can see the gray streaks of a distant rain shower which never reaches us. As the sky turns pearly in the lowering light, we get back into the canoe to paddle back to camp, the water transforming from its usual muddy brown into reflected purples edged with gold. Like a perfect movie ending to a perfect day, we sail back into the setting sun.

Searching for dolphins

Tuesday: Early Morning Birdwatching - Morning Butterflies - Afternoon Walk To Find Iguanas

Ashuco is pointing up through the lacy acacia tree at a little euphonia bird. The fronds of the acacia are still closed up for the night since it's only 6 AM. As the sun rises, the little comb-like fronds will open up like dragonfly wings to absorb the sunlight. I can recognize the squawking of a little flock of parakeets as they fly over, their gossipy voices overlapping as they talk over each other. High on a bare branch, the stately roadside hawk sits silently looking for breakfast. His cousin, the snail kite soars high above us, graceful in his element of air, riding an updraft. My mind turns towards this unseen element. I think of the air's commonality with spirit, an invisible element that supports our own flight through life. The currents of spirit that we need to sense and work with in order to progress. Just as the air carries the piping birdsong, spirit can also carry the messages we need to hear. We just need to pay attention.

"Listen," Ashuco says excitedly. Calling my attention to some high gurgling notes while he points out the tiny barbet who is calling. I hear the zinging flight of the hummingbird first and point it out to him. The hummingbird is joined by two other of his fellows and they go zipping off, laughing and teasing each other.

We leave our little plank road that we travel every day, to loop off to the side. I am delighted to see the farm where folks had been threshing rice, and their open-sided, palm thatched platform where they store their sacks of rice. By their house, Ashuco points out the "acai palm" from which, he explains, they obtain the "heart of palm" that is sold in our supermarkets. I also recognize the name from the super-nutritious dried fruit that is sold in the health food stores. Next to that, Ashuco

identifies a type of palm with arching
sprays of small round fruits that he says
are used to produce a black dye. There is
also a small fruiting pineapple, planted like
an ornamental bush by the farmer's
porch.

For a bit, we watch a male oropendola
bird as he is working on attracting a
female. He sits on a bare branch where
he can be well seen, dipping down his
head, and spreading out his wings like he
is flipping out a cloak dramatically behind
him, showing off the yellow underside of
his tail. He makes a liquid melodic water-
drip sound. "Aren't I handsome?" he
asks. "Look at my glossy, black feathers!
I am strong and will make beautiful babies!
Look at me!"

We leave him to his courting and loop
around on the other side of the path,
passing the old farmer with his wide
brimmed hat, off to harvest more rice.
Ashuco points out a "solitary cacique"
bird, a "white-eared" solitaire (having two

white spots on either side of its head,)
and two black-capped mocking thrushes
singing a loving antiphonal duet to each
other. "You are my only..."
"Yes, my only..."
"Love, I love you..."
"Yes, I do too..."

We stop at a tree that has had two chips
of bark taken off exposing the pale inner
wood and it is oozing a reddish resin.
Ashuco says its name which sound likes
"yodon" to me. He informs me that the
resin is good for stopping bleeding right
away and for soothing itching. I'm not
sure if it acts more like an anti-coagulant
or just like a Bandaid with the thick sticky
resin. Ashuco says it's part of the
pharmacy of the jungle. He dabs his
finger in the sap and has me sniff the
strong but pleasantly spicy scent.

We are distracted by a bright flash of
color and follow it through the trees to
see a colorful toucan perch on a branch as
two others fly by. After the toucan flies

off, Ashuco flashes a big grin and gives me a high five. It certainly was the highlight of the morning! Three big beautiful toucans!

We meander back towards camp, watching a small troop of marmoset monkeys clamber around a large tree, then one-by-one go leaping to the branch of a neighboring tree on their little sky bridge.
"Follow me! This way!"
There are about ten to fifteen of the nimble little critters. I am surprised to see our jungle path emerges right behind our cabins, which is wonderful because the day is heating up quickly. I rinse the sweat off in a morning shower, and happily join my daughter at breakfast, enjoying a fruit compote with some sort of creamy sweet sauce.

After going through the Birds of Peru book, Ashuco points out many of the birds that we have spotted in our week here:

white-winged parakeet, cobalt-winged
parakeet, blue-winged parakeet,
dusky-headed parakeet, blue & yellow
macaw, large-billed tern, wattled jacana,
turkey vulture, yellow-headed vulture,
snail kite, red-throated caracara falcon,
the teeny yellow & blue euphonia, red-
breasted blackbird, yellow-hooded
blackbird, yellow-rumped cacique, solitary
cacique, cotinga, oropendola, red-capped
cardinal, chestnut-bellied seedeater, lined
seedeater, blue-gray tanager, silver-
beaked tanager, coraya wren, buff-
breasted wren, white-bearded manakin,
cotinga, masked tityra, tropical kingbird,
boat-billed flycatcher, great flycatcher,
social flycatcher (which live all together in
a great big nest!), tody-flycatcher, white-
shouldered antbird, plumbeous antbird,
hornero, spinetail, the impressive crimson-
crested woodpecker, chestnut
woodpecker, cream-colored woodpecker,
spot-breasted woodpecker, yellow-tufted
woodpecker, piculet, white-throated
toucan, toucanette scarlet-crowned
barbet, white-eared jacamar, paradise

jacamar, ringed kingfisher (that we saw fishing at the treehouse), Amazon kingfisher (the smaller kind on the banks of the river), black-tailed trogon, green-backed trogon, glittering-throated emerald hummingbird, the nocturnal hermit bird, great potoo, Amazonian pygmy owl, and screech owl.

Later on, I read that Theodore Parker III, a famous American ornithologist once said "Peru offers 'bird enthusiasts' more than any other country in the world... Being here is like being a child visiting a huge store filled with new and fascinating toys." The reason for this is Peru has over 1,800 species of birds with more being discovered each year! It has been described as a country with "more bird species than found in all of North America and Europe combined."

Oropendola

After breakfast we set off to see the
Butterfly Farm, "For de mom," as Ashuco
says. We turn off our boardwalk path,
going past our local rice farmer's storage
hut stacked with sacks of rice and a lovely
hand woven basket.

We get to the start of this village's
sidewalk. Apparently someone has been
using part of the sidewalk for threshing
their rice, so we walk on the grass around
the pile. We follow the sidewalk until it
comes to a large ravine where the remains
of a trestle bridge lay tossed about like a
giant's toy. It is apparently the work of
the flooding Amazon and its tributary.
This now traces innocuously along the
bottom of the ravine, an innocent looking
(half meter) two-feet-across streamlet.
In the past, someone had made some log
steps going down the steep bank, but
they also have been washed out. Instead,
we have to travel down a mud path with a
hairpin curve. We get to a spot where
they had taken two of the timbers from
the former bridge and formed a rickety

little bridge across. We climb up the bank with the remains of the ruined trestle bridge rising crookedly beside us. When we get to the top we pick back up the sidewalk. It leads into a village with its customary rectangular, grassy central area around which buildings are set.

This is the first time we see any construction not made out of wood or palm. Apparently the local missionaries had built a cinderblock-type church and some schools. We can hear the children inside chattering away. It is far noisier than any school I had ever gone to. A few girls in polyester plaid skirts and cotton blouses pass us on the sidewalk giggling. I entertain stormy thoughts about those who would confine these free-spirited jungle children in boxes of cinderblock and clothes of swelteringly hot polyester.

We see our first public "telephonica." It is under a porch roof on the outside of a board building. They have very reasonable rates with local calls priced at .20 soles for a minute (about 7 cents.) Of course, that's if the people you are calling have a phone... and electricity...

We pass two chickens contently perching on a rusty, broken wheelbarrow in the shade of a palm, with brilliant jungle flowers cascading around them. The hens barely take any notice of us and continue on with their private muttered conversation.

In this village is the first time I see a water catchment system. It startles me into wondering why haven't I seen more? Most of the water seems to be hauled by hand from the muddy streamlets or from the Amazon. The water catchment seems like a much better way to get fresh water. This one has a V-shaped little wooden gutter down under the edge of their roof, lined with re-used plastic bags, where it then pours into a large blue plastic barrel (like a pickle barrel.) The barrel had a clean piece of material spread over the top and fastened to keep out any insects and filter the water. I don't understand why all the houses don't have this.

Ashuco points out a "kapok cotton" tree, with tufts of cottony fiber. He reminds us that the Yagua had used this on the end of their blow darts. He identifies some fruiting coconut trees (although the fruits look unfamiliar to me with a smooth shell and a pale orange color) and a tall banana tree with green, ripening bananas hanging down in a huge bunch. A nearby cactus stands about five feet tall. It catches my eye because someone had drawn graffiti on it. I can make out the initials "TGM" carved into the flat surface, the cuts now brown, show up against the bright green of the smooth flat cactus. Under the initials it says, "Te amo mi amor," signed "Pedro."
"I love you, my Love"
... Graffiti the expression of young lovers everywhere!

We turn to our left and cross another trestle bridge that somehow survived the floods, although I can see where bits of the railing had been knocked out, probably by floating logs. This leads us to a well-manicured grassy avenue, flanked by regularly planted palm trees and a beautiful yellow-flowering hedge.

We turned again at a sign, in which I can make out "10 species de mariposas" (ten species of butterflies) and "en la region Loreto" (in the region of Loreto) and that it is protected. Rising up on either side of us are huge, black-netted "screen houses," each with a black-netted "vestibule" in order to enter and not let out the butterflies.

We follow Ashuco into one of the tents, which has lots of Oedipus owl butterflies. The butterflies are large and brown with "eye spots" when they are sitting with their wings closed, but when they flutter around I can see a deep blue shimmer on the backs of their wings. Ashuco directs our attention to the trees growing in there and points out the shriveled brown leaves at their edges. These are actually the caterpillars! Even after we can spy the little antenna on the caterpillars, it is *still* hard to believe that it isn't a bit of shriveled up leaf.

We leave the butterfly house and head for a wooden building at the end of the row of screen houses. Apparently the butterfly researcher isn't in, but Ashuco has been here often enough to be able to summarize things for us. In the one-room wooden building are shelves of clear plastic containers (like you might get at the Chinese restaurant with your soup in it.) In each of these, are the pupae of the butterflies and in some are fluttering butterflies that must have just emerged. Ashuco explains that the scientist here is studying the wasps that prey upon the butterflies, among other things. We get to see a shimmering blue and black "morpho helenor", one that is striped orange and black like a tiger, another orange and black one that looks like a cross between the tiger one and a monarch, a few that are brown and almost totally camouflaged, but all of them beautiful!

We leave the scientist's room and walk around to a huge, circular screen house that borders a pond. It is full of the Oedipus Owl butterflies. There must be a hundred of them fluttering all around the screen house. Scattered around on poles are little wooden "house-type" bird feeders, but instead they hold some pieces of rotting banana that the butterflies eat. There are trees inside this screen house and plenty of flowers. I sit down on the mossy ground and just let them flutter all around me, their wings whispering mournfully against the screening. "Out. Out. We want to get out. The blue sky is calling us."

It is beautiful to have them fluttering all around me, but it also crosses my mind as

I sit there, that they have everything they need in this screen house, yet most of them spend the day fluttering against the screen trying to get out. They remind me of the school children confined in their cement schoolhouse. I wonder if that list we learned in school of the necessities of life: food, clothing, and shelter, should have included freedom as well.

Cement Schoolhouse

Despite the blazing blue sky and blistering heat, Coriander convinces me to come out with her and Ashuco. I had enjoyed our hot afternoons immersed in the Amazon river looking for dolphins. Although I am disappointed we hadn't seen iguanas the other day, I am feeling a bit reticent to head out in the heat, but with some wheedling on Coriander's part, and remembering to make the most of our last day in the jungle, I join them on their walk.

We take some of the same route as this morning's trip to see the butterflies; walking out our plank road, going past the rice farmer's storage hut, picking up the cement sidewalk, crossing down in the gorge of the ruined bridge, climbing back up to the sidewalk, and on to the village. This time, we walk straight through the village. There is a cement area about as big as a basketball court that is set up with two bare metal goal posts of some kind, but at the moment it is being used for rice threshing. Two men and a boy, shaking the lighter husks free from the rice kernels, piles of rice randomly placed around the "basketball court." We walk past rough-cut board houses painted various shades of weathered pastel. There are a multitude of colorful laundry lines taking advantage of the bright sunlight.

We finally veer off onto a path through cornfields and jungle. A little girl about five sees us and waves cheerily, "Hola, gringas!" We smile back and wave, appreciating her enthusiasm and knowing no offense was meant by the term. We teeter over another "Peruvian bridge" but my perfect record of navigating rickety bridges is spoiled as one foot slips off the log into the water. However, no caimans show up and I regain my footing and cross. A short time later, Ashuco stops. His golden tooth flashing in the sun as he beams at Coriander triumphantly. He silently points up at a large iguana stretching out on a tree branch, its two-and-a-half-feet long tail dangling down.

We exchange high fives all around as we congratulate him on spotting an iguana.

We walk a little bit further, but by that point I have finished my container of water and started on Coriander's. We turn around at a little hut with some calabash trees growing to the side and notice that tucked just under a bush was a baby toucan. I don't know if he lost his nest or was a pet, but we are able to get a photo of him. He makes a funny little hissing/squawking noise when we get too close for his comfort. "Back off! My Mama will get you!" he challenges with bravado twice his size.

On the way back Ashuco seems to have gotten into the groove, because he spots three more iguanas. We safely cross the Peruvian log bridge and then come back to the village. We had observed that jungle chickens had very long muscular legs and this leads us to conclude that this is in order to outrace the jaguars.

Walking back along the village sidewalk, we pass a man carrying a machete. It isn't until I think about it afterwards, that I notice that people carrying machetes has become perfectly normal. It is a reminder that the American "right to carry" gun laws make sense in context; when a machete is used as an every day tool, it's one thing, when it is used to kill someone, it's quite another.

We see a woman out sweeping the bare dirt in front of her house to get rid of any unsightly leaves. That is in big contrast with a few other houses where they seem to completely forget that their plastic wrappers are not going to decompose like most things in the jungle. It gets me musing on their lifestyle which is a very temporary one. Things aren't built for perfection or to last forever. The powerful Amazon river can just flood and wipe it all away, and they just seem to go with it and make everything temporary. Their makeshift staircases up the river banks, which will have to be rebuilt once or twice a year, their "Peruvian bridges" built of logs and tied with vines or a frayed bit of scrap rope, their slapped-together, open-air, rough-cut houses... it is a life that accepts impermanence and lives in rhythm with the natural cycles. It is as if their whole life is the practice of aikido, the gentle flow of absorbing the energy coming at you and shaping it as it flows back out.

As we walk back we can hear the far off rumble of a thunderstorm brewing. When we get to the cabin, I am delighted to cool off with my third cold shower of the day. We lay on our beds and rest in the heat listening to the increasing rumble of thunder until a marvelous breeze whips up and brings in the evening rain accompanied by some beautiful lightning strikes rippling across the sky. The breezes coming in are awesome, billowing out our privacy curtains like restless ghosts. The tiny tree frogs are peeping and it almost sounds like the chiming of little bells in the night.

We pack everything up since we are leaving in the wee hours of the morning. Coriander shakes her humid and frizzy long hair that has been washed in brown Amazon water each night. She consoles herself about leaving with the comment, "I can't wait to go home and have hair that looks like mine again. I've just had this nasty jungle stuff on my head."

"Then again," she adds, thinking of the crime-laden city of Iquitos, "There's just something about coming out of the jungle, all muddy and sweaty. 'I wrestled an anaconda and fought off monkey pick-pockets. You don't scare me!'"
She makes a fearsome face at me and I laugh.

As we are lying in bed ready to sleep, Coriander remarks in a satisfied way, "After just a week I can lie here and listen to the calls and say, that's a screech owl, that's a jungle rat, that's a potoo."

"Mmm," I agree sleepily. Thinking wistfully as I drift into sleep, I will miss their voices.

The Search for Iguanas

Wednesday: Early Boat Trip To Iquitos - The Iquitos Market - Arrive in Lima, Peru - Kennedy Park - Cacao Museo and Bonbons

I wake up at 3:30 AM and lay silently listening to the jungle noises, absorbing these last moments in the jungle; the hollow "chuck, chuck, chuck" of the bamboo rat, the peeping of frogs, and the trill of a screech owl. "Farewell. Farewell. We shall still be here should you return. Remember us." I promise them silently that I will not forget them.

Then it is a matter of getting dressed and dragging out our bags that we had packed the night before. We are out the door by 4 AM and carry our bags to the beginning of our plank walkway. Ashuco asks if I have my walking stick, because it had rained in the evening and the boards were wet and slippery. When I say I forgot it, he swiftly walks back to the cabin and gets it for me.

While the guides pull together the luggage
for us and the Korean lady who was also
leaving, Coriander and I walk by the light
of the flashlight along the random
network of planks, stumps, and logs down
to the river (and I am very thankful to
Ashuco for my stick!) We finally get to
see the stars fairly clearly for the first
time this whole week. Orion is certainly
tipped more sideways and we can pick out
the Pleiades. It makes my heart lighter to
greet familiar stars connecting me to
home.

Once on the boat, Coriander snuggles
under my sweater and flannel shirt. (I
haven't used them all week but because
they didn't fit in my bag I had tied them
around my waist.) She settles down on
her airplane neck pillow, pulls her bandana
down over her eyes, and snoozes for
most of the two-hour boat ride. I am too
excited to sleep, wanting to squeeze out
every last minute of our time in the
Amazon. At first the land is a just a black

silhouette, with the deep gray water and gray sky that our boat moves into, but after a bit, things began to lighten. We pass a whole bunch of garish lights illuminating a huge gas tanker named after the river Curaray, but ironically sounding like the poison "curare."

Ashuco's job has been to sit up front, shining a flashlight on occasion to make sure the boat didn't bump into any submerged logs, but after it gets lighter, he lies back and naps a little. The sun breaks out over the horizon of the Amazon river adding a beautiful pink glow to the last bit of our ride. When Ashuco stretches and gets back up, the other guide teases him with a sassy, "Buenos dias!"

We squeeze in a few more bird sightings. Ashuco excitedly pointing out a bat falcon flying by. He explains that they eat the nocturnal bats. Presumably it is getting back home from its nighttime hunting. We also see some busy woodpeckers and an Amazon kingfisher hunting for breakfast. On a high branch, the liquid-trilling oropendola bows towards me, flipping out its dark wings and nodding a last farewell. As the boat motors towards the noisy town the jungle voices are drowned out.

We approach the collection of tin roofed shacks that surrounds our harbor at Iquitos. I guess Maniti tours has an arrangement with the floating bar there, because we pull in next to it and tie our boat up to it. We climb aboard the floating building with its posters of beer, and large empty room at 6 AM. Ashuco insists on carrying our bags. He loads up with my strapped suitcase as a front pack, Coriander's suitcase as a backpack and holds his own backpack on his head. We all have to laugh when his phone rings somewhere under all that, but he skillfully manages to extricate it from his jean pocket and answer it.

We wind up standing there at the end of the floating building, because for some reason in the night, their network of floating gangplanks got all tangled and tossed on top of one another. I feel sorry for Ashuco standing there under all that luggage, but he looks as cool as a cucumber just like he has all week.

A worker at the floating bar finally straightens it out, and we progress up a series of planks that keep us out of the plastic grocery bag and rubbish filled mud that comprises this side of the Amazon river.

We emerge into the same colorful, bustling farmers' market: melons, bananas, live chickens, dead chickens, fish, peppers, and people walking around and selling. We don't see our lady with toasted grubs on a stick. (I think to Coriander's relief because she is still looking sleepy and not at all adventurous!) We emerge onto the street on the other side of this little market and into the cluster of tuk-tuks. Our fellow guest gets into one, and we wish her well as she goes off to catch her flight. Since our flight leaves a few hours later, that gives us some time to check out Iquitos in Ashuco's safe company.

Ashuco engages a tuk-tuk driver for us. This is the first time we are actually riding in one, rather than just looking at them zipping about on the road around us. The driver sits on the front of a motorcycle but instead of a back wheel, there is a small cart attached, turning it into a three-wheeled conveyance. The cart just has a bench seat and a roof, no doors, no windows. Our luggage goes into a wire rack on the back, and the three of us squeeze in tightly together on the bench seat behind the motorcycle driver's seat. With his backpack in his lap, Ashuco reaches through the non-existent back window to hold onto my bag, and Coriander holds onto hers and off we fly!

After a few minutes of navigating the madness of the traffic, Coriander looks at me all wide-eyed and says, "Who needs coffee when you have adrenalin?!" There still seems to be no rules of the road except for a grudging concession for red lights. The tuk-tuks all roaringly race at breakneck speed, weaving in and out. The double lane roads are marked for two cars across but that doesn't apply to tuk-tuks or motorcycles, and they just follow their own crazy combinations. We weave in and out of the roaring cacophony, past big delivery trucks spewing thick exhaust. I have no idea where they are all going at 6 o'clock in the morning, but perhaps everyone commutes early to avoid the mid-day heat.

We finally arrive at the Maniti office. Coriander tries to let go of her bag and is surprised to find she can't. She finally manages to unclench her fingers, commenting, "I now know what the term 'white-knuckled' means!"

Ashuco unlocks the big iron gate out front and the heavy wooden inner door so we can enter the relative calm of their office. We tuck our bags safely in the back room. Ashuco insists that Coriander leaves her large professional camera here because it will certainly get snatched in the market place. He advises us to hold on tightly to our little iPhones if we want to take pictures.

We use their internet to assure family that we have survived the jungle (not mentioning that we are venturing out into a place much more dangerous than we had been all week) and set out with Ashuco leading the way.

A pecamari

It is very reassuring to be in Ashuco's company because you could just see the contrast of our wiry, muscled jungle guides compared to the slightly beer-bellied or scrawny city dwellers. Ashuco walks with a confident stride ahead of us, leading us to a bedraggled area that looks like a sort of Victorian English promenade beside the marshy part of the river. It reminds me of the description of Miss Havisham's wedding gown in Dickens' book, Great Expectations; this fine, elaborate gown that has now all gone to ruin.

We hear a "Hola!" and an older man stops to chat with Ashuco, shaking our hands in greeting and happily talking full speed in Spanish. We take the opportunity to look around while they are chatting away. What used to be a promenade with a white painted cement banister looking over the grassy lower lands that flood from the Amazon, now looks over a derelict touring steamboat that was stranded in the marshlands. The sad ruin of a boat has palm trees growing through it and is rusting away. A little further away from us, on the edge of the marsh is a tin-roofed shanty town. The white painted banisters of the promenade are peeling and weathered, the one grand Victorian hotel across the street, has iron bars on the lower windows, with cracked decorative tiles and peeling paint distracting from the once glorious elaborate ironwork balconies, and room-high windows that opened out onto the view. However, some blossoming trees cheer up the avenue and we try to ignore the soldiers that have turned these blocks of hotels into a barracks.

It is a sad, sad history, the Era of the Rubber Barons and a sad ending to it that we were currently walking through, stepping over the cracked and broken paving stones of this Victorian promenade.

When Ashuco's friend leaves, we start walking again. Coriander asks in an amazed voice, "Ashuco, do you know everyone?!" making him laugh. We eventually get to the long and busy main street of their market. It is a barrage of sensations; the bright colors of all the vegetables; a rainbow of peppers, fruits, huge bunches of bananas, with stooped and weathered brown Peruvians carrying pounds of them on their back and head. The people are chattering back and forth and calling out about their wares, like the squawking of a flock of parakeets.

The scents of motorcycle exhaust, damp cellars, sweet fresh fruit, tangy spices, and pungent meat is all around us. The stalls are set up all along the sides of the street with a space narrow enough to fit two or three people (or the occasional motorcycle!) We see several people selling oils, vinegars, and other sauces packaged in tube-like, clear plastic bags hung up in clusters like fruiting bananas. We also see unlabeled spices in narrow plastic bags as well. There are women with carts full of little purple-scaled fruits that look like mini-dragon eggs. They peel the small egg-sized fruit to show the lovely juicy mango-orange underneath. I find out later it's called an aguaje. It comes from the Moriche palm which is native to the Peruvian Amazon and is very nutritious.

There are tables full of fish for sale including the beautifully striped "tiger catfish" that had been cooked so tender for our dinner one night in the jungle. Next to that are several baskets of "walking catfish", many of them still flapping vainly in the woven reed basket. We see rows of turtle cut up for soup, their clawed, detached legs still recognizable, their shells taken off to use elsewhere. There are also butchered caiman alligators, their clawed feet limply hanging over the edge of the table. In some places the smells are rather powerful. In all of that long street, I only saw one stall that had its seafood on crushed ice. This is only seven in the morning and I shudder to think how it will reek under the full mid-day tropical sun.

Ashuco guides us through the major meat section where some people specialize in just beef stomach or only liver. I confess, I am very glad to leave that area. Ashuco leads us further down the street and into an interesting side street that he explains is the herbs and medicines. It smells much better! I even recognize a few of the medicine trees that Ashuco had pointed out on our walks. There are little piles of sticks of the medicinal wood, bundles of bark, bundles of fresh herbs, incense, and even rows of dark bottles with handmade decoctions. I find it a very interesting section.

There are lots of thin, stray dogs walking around the street, but only a few cats. We observe one enterprising cat on the table behind the fishmonger, trying to drag off its ill-gotten gains, inspiring Coriander to come up with the expression of "happier than a cat in a Peruvian fish market."

Three woman sit at a booth where they are hand-rolling cigarettes, and the stacked piles of finished cigarettes tower up next to them; the round graduated bundles stacked up like a layered wedding cake. It reminds me that we really hadn't come across anyone smoking. In France or Italy, this type of market would have me trying to avoid clouds of smoke, but aside from our Shaman using them in ritual, and one morning where Ashuco smoked one to "chase away de mosquitos" I don't think we saw anyone else smoking in Peru.

We pass a building that had an empty warehouse with a dirt floor. Next to it is a storefront of plywood painted with a cartoon of a happy tooth. We can't see inside the dental office, but considering the neighborhood I shudder to think of getting dental work done here. Finally, we come to the end of the street with the waters of the Amazon before us. The hill is a tangled heap of trash. Ashuco says in his broken English, "De people here, dey throw away junk, theenk de Amazon can hold it all. Eet go down to de jungle. Go down to my home. De reever can never hold it all." We agree it is terrible and hope that a solution can be found. I wish they would institute a bottle deposit, because I'm sure many poor people could benefit from it, and it would clean up about half the trash we see around.

We turn around and start back up the hill. This time I look more at the people than their wares. Although I think of myself as average height at 5 feet 4 inches, or maybe a bit on the short side, I realize we are actually among the tallest people there. I see several woman about a head shorter than Coriander at her 5 feet 2 inches. Although we had tried to blend in with our clothing, our skin, several shades lighter than everyone else, stands out. I see one man try to "tease the gringas" by pushing another man into me, but I step quick, and manage to avoid them. It is reassuring to have Ashuco right nearby, but I don't get as many photos as I would like, trying to continuously hide my camera. I have it in a pouch around my neck, and tuck it down under my shirt, so it isn't easy to pull out quickly.

We emerge from the crowded booths of the market into crazy traffic. I only saw one woman riding a motorcycle with a helmet. They seem to have no fear. I see a girl in a mini-skirt riding "side-saddle" behind her boyfriend, looking like she might slide off any minute. Going too fast to take a picture, I spy a two-year-old toddler standing on the motorcycle seat between her mom and dad as they zip around the corner. It almost made the crazy tuk-tuks feel safer.

Away from the market, there is a bit more of the type of shops that you might see anywhere, but Coriander has to stop to take a photo at the tailors shop. Inside, the walls are covered in stacks of fabric, with two older men bent over their work. Out in front was a truly frightening grinning mannequin, supposedly inviting people to come in by showing off the wares, but with its rictus-like grin, I thought it did a better job of scaring off customers.

The day is warming swiftly and I am really feeling it as we walk back to the Maniti office. Ashuco asks, "Hungry?" Coriander rolls her eyes at him, "I'm always hungry, remember?!" Ashuco leads us to a restaurant along the way for breakfast. Ashuco says he isn't hungry, so he just orders a coffee and a beer. When Coriander teases him for being a pirate (at her local Renaissance Festival in Maryland, the saying is that if you drink before 10 AM, you're not a drunk, you're just a pirate.) Ashuco just laughs showing off his pirate-like gold tooth. He says doesn't drink a bunch like some of the other guys, "jeest one." He says he has been coming here for a long time and most of the waitresses know him, but it also seems like Ashuco knows everyone! If we were in the jungle, he'd stop to chat with a native, when we were in the city, people would call out greetings to him or stop by and shake his hand.

I am hot from the strong sun and all the walking, so I order icy coconut milk, served in the shell with a straw, with just a tiny bit of the top chopped off. In the heat of the day it is heavenly, and I hug the cold shell to help lower my body temperature. Apparently, there are different kinds of coconuts in the Amazon because this one is smooth and not "hairy" like the coconuts in the U.S. supermarkets, plus the meat is only about a quarter inch thick, very tender and not "woody" at all. I had seen the smooth skinned coconuts growing in the jungle, but I had thought they were just immature and would develop the "hair" later. I jokingly ask Ashuco if he could borrow their machete and chop it in half for me, so I could eat out the meat. He asks the waitress in Spanish to chop it in half. When she brings it back, Ashuco scoops out the tender meat for me and Coriander, and we nibble the small amount of soft coconut inside. The cafe' is decorated with jungle fish and caiman carved out of wood. One glittering wall-length glass display case shows brightly decorated cakes that almost don't look real!

After that, we walk back to the Maniti office and with the time we have left, we use their wifi to post up a few pictures. The manager there sends for a tuk-tuk for us. When it shows up Ashuco loads up our bags, and it is time for our goodbyes and hugs before Coriander and I take off into the hot and noisy maelstrom which is Iquitos traffic.

On the way in, we were too tired and bewildered to take much in the way of pictures, but on the way out I manage a few photos and a little video to try to capture the experience of the chaos. It does not, however, capture me clutching my feathered blowpipe and "Indiana Jones" hat, the smells of exhaust, muggy heat and the hot, dusty roadway that is part of the sensory overload that is Iquitos.

Iquitos Market

We get to our flight in plenty of time. The lady at the airport desk is probably well acquainted with guests bringing back blowpipes. She tells me that the darts need to be packed away and the bag checked. This gets me a little derailed because I had been planning on carrying it on the plane, and I forget that I have my flip-flops and my journal that I had been writing in all week in a loose outer pocket. With a sinking feeling, I remember this much too late on the plane. I resign myself and trust to luck that it doesn't fall out.

Our flight on Star Peru goes pretty well and we get into Lima around 2 PM. I heave a huge sigh of relief when I see my bag come through the conveyor belt with my little journal just barely held in by the backpack straps. The flip-flops are gone, but I'm so happy to see my journal I don't even worry about the shoes. We just grab our bags and exit the baggage area. This time we ignore anyone asking us anything and just look for a person holding our name card, which we are happy to find right away.

We had arranged for a ride to our hotel with the company, "Local Peruvian Friend" who will be doing our tour the next day. Our driver introduces himself as Alonzo, much to my delight as a Doctor Who fan! I restrain myself from saying, "Allons-y, Alonzo," because I don't want to scare our driver with random movie quotes. We had been very lucky that Ashuco put up with all of our weird and off-hand comments and joked right along, now we had to rein in our natural tendencies and act like normal people. It turns out that Alonzo is not going to be our guide the next day. He tells us he works in their office and just came out to pick us up. Our guide the next day was going to be Mariela.

Alonzo gives us a few school-like facts about the city as we drive. The population in Lima has doubled in the past twenty years and they are seeing a lot of development. We can see the amount of construction going on all around us, new hotels by the sea, the lovely landscaped highways we are traveling on, and lots of traffic. Alonzo explains that Lima is divided into different sections, each with its own mayor and all of them under one "regional president mayor." He warns us that each of the sections has its own taxi rate, so I am glad we are having the tour company drive us around the next day. He mentions that the area, Miraflores, that we had picked to stay in is a very good area. As well as the regular police, it has its own private police force. Lima certainly seems to be a city of contradictions; safe and dangerous, ancient and new.

We had looked online and picked the "Hotel Antigua Miraflores" which is near a large park, and even though it is in a built-up part of the city, there is supposed to be an ancient temple nearby. Alonzo asks us if we like cats, and Coriander quickly agrees, so he suggests we should visit

Kennedy Park, a short walking distance from our hotel. He points out the direction the park as he drops us off at a brightly painted yellow and orange stuccoed "hacienda." It has a wrought iron privacy gate that we need to be buzzed in through.

Our hotel feels like a beautiful oasis, with a restful green courtyard out front, artfully placed amphoras, and lovely landscaped flowers. The front door is open and inside is a large tiled area with white and black tiles forming diamond patterns on the floor. A carved and polished wood front desk exudes a timeless elegance. The clerk mentions that we have a free upgrade, which we find out means the room is larger with an extra bed, the downside is that it is way up on the fourth floor with no elevator and all the way towards the back. However, the bell-boy helps us with our luggage and the steps are broad with landings. There is no air-conditioning that we can tell, but every time we checked online Lima's seaside temperature had seemed to be a steady 70 degrees (21 Celsius) or so. The stairway windows are all open wide with no screens, the interior windows have a curling wrought-iron grill through which we look down on a lovely interior courtyard with a gently cascading fountain. Each staircase landing has a water cooler, and I make a mental note to come back and refill our empty water bottles.

Our room is large and lovely, and I feel like an intruder kicking off my muddy boots under the elegant Spanish stretched leather chair, putting down my battered hat next to their artfully crafted lamp made from an antique flatiron, and plunking the primitive blowpipe on the polished desk. Coriander dashes to check out the bathroom and I hear a happy little squeal. Poking in my head, I see her standing there in a elegantly tiled room half the size of our jungle cabin, doing a little happy dance.

"There's a *seat* on the toilet!... And a shower curtain!" She exclaims in ecstasy.

I leave her to a long shower, and pull out a few damp items of jungle clothing from my bag, that I knew hadn't had time to dry. "Phew!" I exclaim, as the scent of sweat and damp bathing suit hits me. The windows are open and letting in a lovely breeze, so I drape the clothes over the window sill to completely dry.

I get a shower after my daughter and emerge scented with flower shampoo and feeling un-sticky for the first time in a week. Coriander calls my attention to a little printed card, "FREE SHOESHINE, Ask at the front desk." She chuckles mischievously and looks at her muddy, battered, grayish boots. "I don't think they were counting on someone coming out of the jungle," she laughs. "Do you think they'll do them?" I dig through my tummy pack and come up with a combination of an American dollar and some Peruvian coins, which is all the money I have left. "Here, that ought to be a good enough tip."

We wend our way back down again to the front desk. It turns out that our bellboy is also the shoe-shine fellow. We ask if it's still okay to get some lunch here at the hotel, as we've lost track of time. It seems somewhere in the vicinity of three or four o'clock and we've had no lunch. The hotel manager assures us that would be fine. If Coriander would like to leave her boots and the tip at the desk, she can go sock-footed to the little "bar" dining area. The fellow there could take our lunch order and her shoes would be finished by the time we are done. That all works for us!

Trying to experience the most of Peru, Coriander orders octopus (pulpi) and I order quinoa croquettes. Quinoa is a grain that originated in the Andes region of Peru. We pronounce it as "KEEN-wah" in the states, but in the Andean Quecha language it is pronounced as "kee-NOO-

ah." But however it is pronounced it is all awesomely delicious. The portions are a bit small for two starving travelers, but enough to tide us over until dinner.
When we are done, the manager brings Coriander some glistening black boots that bear only a bit of resemblance to the footwear that was given them. The bell-boy had even polished the laces!
Coriander grins from ear to ear and dons her revived footwear. We find an area map in the lobby and head out in the direction of Kennedy Park and cats.

Hotel Antigua Miraflores

According to the map, it is a slightly zig-zaggy route to the park, the roads being laid out more like a spiderweb than a grid. We pass a man who seems to be negotiating with a taxi driver. He turns to us and asks us something in Spanish, which we don't understand. We just say no and shake our heads. He asks again more insistently and Coriander firmly says, "No!" and we walk on by. He gives a screech like a three-year-old having a temper tantrum and Coriander said when she looked back he was angrily giving us the finger. There is a bookstore right there and we quickly take refuge inside.

Perusing for a little bit, I select a children's book on the Incas and Coriander picks out one in Spanish on folk tales. I'd have lingered longer in the book store but Coriander points out that the sun will be going down soon, so we should get going. We quick check our directions while we are inside the bookstore (not wanting to be marked out as tourists on the street.)

We only have to walk two more streets and we arrive at Kennedy Park.

And it is *full* of cats. I have no idea why this block of city developed as a cat haven, but we do see a lady off to the side feeding the cats. They are wandering around the sidewalks, perching lazily in trees, sitting in the grass, and lounging on the benches. At the entrance is a nine feet tall (three meter) Peruvian pot and in the middle of the park, on a cement pedestal, is a bronze bust of John F. Kennedy. We puzzle about this for a while, as Coriander sits on the ground and has a kitty snuggle up to her legs, finally filing the question away as "something we need to look up later." There is also a business (maybe a restaurant) that has life size effigies of Charlie Chaplin and John Wayne. When Coriander comments on the crazy combination, I shrug and say that I could imagine a Mexican restaurant in the U.S. having a statue of Pancho Villa next to Frida Kahlo and a Mexican traveler might be perplexed as to why.

Kennedy Park

When Coriander has gotten her daily dose of kitty cuteness, we start zig-zagging back, taking a slightly different path, only to serendipitously stumble upon the Cacao Museo!

The museum is a glass fronted business that advertises in English, "Free Chocolate Tours." Well... that doesn't need much discussion! We make a beeline across the street for it. We are greeted by a lovely Peruvian girl, Stephanie, who gives us a sample of cocoa tea, made from the husks of the cocoa bean. It is delicious. She leads us through their three-room exhibit of cocoa, with a sculpted cacao tree. We tell her we had just seen the real deal in the jungle. Stephanie informs us that the best cocoa pods came from the trunk of the tree, rather than the ones that grow from the branches, which we didn't know. I had grown up near the town of Hershey, PA, and Coriander had recently visited Theo chocolate factory in Oregon, so we are pretty well versed in the chocolate process. It is still neat seeing the process in the land where the cocoa beans come from.

Stephanie says that after extracting the cocoa mass, they process it with liquid in a churning process that takes two days! They have about twenty bottles of different chocolate liquors set out and about twenty jars of "chocolate jam" made with chocolate and fruit. She is perfectly happy to give us samples of all of them, but we limit our taste testing to about three of each (figuring if we had sips of all the liquors, we might not be able to find our way back to the hotel!) Keeping in mind airline regulations, we each get a tiny bottle of our favorite chocolate liquor and a bag of cocoa tea. The jams are interesting, especially the ones made with specifically Peruvian fruit like aguaje or lúcuma, but we skip getting any of those and instead get assorted chocolate truffles, and at Coriander's insistence, "bonbons."

"I've never had 'bonbons' and I want to be able to say we went back to our hotel and had 'bonbons!'" she says.

I laugh knowing it's just another name for a small candy treat. These are different flavors of chocolate wrapped in foil. Our indulgences and gifts cost us about 60 soles altogether (or about ten dollars each.) Now it is just starting to get dark, so we scamper back to the hotel.

Forget dessert... we decide to have the "bonbons" and truffles as appetizers, and it is some of the best chocolate we've ever had. It is hard to believe that we started our day walking through mud, swatting away mosquitos in the jungle, and now we are sitting on plush and cushy beds in a luxurious hotel eating bonbons!

I look over our little area map and determine that the oval spot labeled "Huaca Pucllana" is probably the ancient archeological site. It is on the same street as our hotel, just seven blocks away. Looking online confirms that it is the ruins of the Temple of the Moon with surrounding buildings, and that Huaca Pucllana opened at nine in the morning. That gave us just enough time tomorrow to walk there, tour it (and maybe get some more bonbons at the Cacao Museo on the way back) and check out of the hotel at eleven o'clock when Mariela was scheduled to meet us.

We decide the safest course of action is to dine in the hotel, even if it is a tad more expensive than an outside restaurant. Seeing the barbed wire, and the broken glass topping the walls and rooftops around town, we figure it is worth it for the safety.

After dinner, I start looking up more information on Iquitos and the rubber barons, and I start telling Coriander about some of the information I just read.

"It was a terrible time and a shameful history for Europeans. You know that rubber really took off when Goodyear discovered the process of vulcanization. Well, they discovered a lot of rubber trees in Peru and that's why Iquitos became such a boom town deep in the Amazon jungle. The Europeans hired some of the elite mestizos, the ones descended from the Spanish conquistadors, and put them in charge. They got thugs to capture the natives, like the Yagua tribe we met, and forced them to gather huge balls of rubber that were to be delivered to the town. If the balls didn't weigh enough, the men were savagely beaten and often killed. If a male slave escaped, his wife was raped and his children were beaten and tortured." I said sadly.

"That's awful," Coriander comments. "Yeah," I said, "And you saw how the natives lived. They weren't used to doing hard labor from sun up to sun down. They're used the easy ebb and flow of the jungle, fishing when they are hungry, gathering fruit when they feel like it and resting in the warm afternoons. Hundreds of thousands of natives were killed and some hid deep in the jungle, like the Yaguas, which is why some of their tribe still survive. At this time the Europeans were prospering from the slave labor tremendously, the people in control became millionaires, which is why you can see all the beautiful Victorian buildings that were built. The wealth inequality was staggering. But the Rubber Boom ended around 1920, which is why all the grand old buildings look like they are falling apart in Iquitos."

"At least they don't do that anymore," said Coriander.
"Well, no... and yes. Certainly the oil exploration is likely to turn into exploitation of the area. Yes, they'll pay their employees a good wage, especially in a depressed area like Iquitos, but they don't really care about any environmental damage that the Yaguas might suffer because of it."
Coriander nods sadly.

"But we can at least do our part to decrease the demand for petroleum products, like using fuel efficient cars, insulating our house, and avoiding lots of plastic packaging. I know you have the good habit of using cloth bags when you go to the supermarket to get groceries and it's at least a start."

"That hardly seems like it's enough," says Coriander, "It's just a drop in the bucket."

"But what is an ocean, but a multitude of drops?" I ask rhetorically, quoting from our favorite movie, Cloud Atlas.

Encourage your friends and we can make a difference."

Kakaw

Thursday: Our Last Day in Peru - The Temple of the Moon at Huaca Pucllana - The Temple of the Sun at Pachacamac - Touring Downtown Lima - The Larco Museum

A breakfast buffet is included at the Hotel Antigua and I find the combination of foods certainly different than a breakfast in the U.S.; eggs, homemade rolls, cheese, ham, cooked mushrooms, and onions. There is yoghurt, but Coriander didn't realize it was to be served as a drink and poured herself a bowl. It is only after she is sitting at the table with me and eating it with a spoon, that she realizes it is a rather thin consistency and everyone else around the room has poured it into a glass. She laughs at what they must think of the "American tourists," but I don't think anyone noticed.

They serve most of the same types of tea as they did at our camp in the jungle, but

not knowing any Spanish they were a
mystery: anis, te canla y clavo,
manzanilla, herba luisa, and coca. Now
with connectivity, we can translate them
and find they are anise, cinnamon & clove,
camomile, lemongrass, and coca leaf. We
didn't have coca tea in the jungle. I had
heard it was a stimulant and used to
adjust to the altitude in the Andes.
Although we are at sea level I figure I'll
give it a try, and I find it very good. On
my way out, I grab an extra bag for my
husband to try. Later I find out that it is
made from the same leaves that they use
to manufacture cocaine, but coca tea is
no more stimulating than black tea.

We pack up everything in our room and
head out to find Huaca Pucllana. When
we had traveled in Italy and the traffic
was horrendous, we found that you just
had to walk confidently across the street
and the traffic would stop. Not so in
Lima! The only thing to do is to wait for a
gap in traffic and then run-for-your-life.
Since there aren't any red lights along our

walk, it is a crazy combination of wait and dash through eight busy streets.

As we get closer, it is fascinating to see this ancient mud-brick structure rising up ahead of us, over the city buildings. We get to the site and find it fenced in. "Pick a direction," I tell Coriander, and off she leads to the left. If we had the little worm from Labyrinth advising us, he'd have agreed with her, because if we had turned right, it would have led us right to the entrance. Instead, we walk around the entire giant structure, finally getting to the entrance around 9:30 AM. This only posed a problem because we're not allowed to look around the site on our own and have to take the guided tour. The Spanish tour is just leaving and the next English tour isn't until 9:45. The tour lasts an hour, which leaves us with just 15 minutes to get back to the hotel, grab our bags, and get downstairs to meet our day's tour guide. We resign ourselves to skipping the Cacao Museo, but at least we can squeeze in this tour at the Temple of the Moon.

While we wait, I examine this impressive expanse of ancient construction rising above me. The dry mud bricks are a dusty, yellowish color, and the feeling of it being a barren desert is accentuated by the few cactus used for landscaping. It stands in stark contrast to the nearby houses that surround it. The city looks much like any other city, hiding the dry desert under sidewalks and landscaping.

The Peruvian tour guide who speaks English, isn't great at it and to compound the problem, gives the impression that she is sick and tired of this job repeating the same old thing over and over. Her lack of enthusiasm really puts a damper on the whole tour. Despite that, we learn that this is a structure built by the original native Lima culture. This pre-Inca culture started around 200 CE, and lasted for 500 years until they were taken over by the Wari culture that conquered most of the costal area. The Lima peoples had two primary deities; Mother Ocean, represented by the shark and the Moon Goddess. This place is now referred to as Huaca Pucllana or the "Place of the Sacred Games," because that seems to have been the original purpose of the huge open platform in the temple area.

We start the tour in a small museum, with a few examples of pottery, some lovely examples of intricate woven baskets, and beautiful textiles. Their pottery is very distinctive, being red clay decorated with black and white. A large red clay urn painted with a stylized shark on it was probably used for offerings to the Ocean Goddess. There is a fascinating example of a comb, which they used long slivers of wood (maybe palm) held in line with woven reeds. The reeds are woven into a lovely diamond pattern. I really enjoy seeing everyday things that the artisan took the time to make them beautiful. They would seem to be a peaceful people, as no weapons were found at the site.

We walk through the ancient administrative center first. The guide explains that this was all to support the temple. There were cooking areas, probably to prepare feasts. There seems to be construction areas where the handmade bricks were shaped and sun-dried.

In analyzing the ancient construction, it looks to have been updated or modified every ten to fifteen years, perhaps when a new ruler came into power. The bricks aren't fired, simply sun-dried and they weren't placed in an overlapping horizontal pattern like we are used to today, but vertically, side-by-side and then slathered with a layer of more mud. On taller walls, the ancient Lima people placed the bricks vertically in tall triangles, let that dry and then came back and filled in the inverted triangles that were left. There are mud-brick ramps and squares surrounded by small buildings and storage rooms. You can still see the imprints of the hands that had formed these bricks almost 2,000 years ago. I wish I could touch these ancient fingerprints, feeling the connection to these people through the veil of time.

We travel around the the side of the ancient administrative area, and come upon a modern movie set, that looks like either it has been teleported in, or the thought occurs to me... perhaps we are walking around the movie set for ancient Peru and just walked back into the "real world." It is all set up with metal scaffolding and fifty feet (fifteen meter) tall black drapery backdrops. There are movie people scampering all over loading or unloading sets, chairs, pipes, and yes, even a kitchen sink! We finally turn a corner and see a gleaming white car set up on a curtained platform surrounded by tables set up like a dining room lounge. Presumably a company had made a large donation to the museum complex and chose to launch their new model of car there.

Leaving the anachronism behind, we cross over into the ceremonial section and begin to walk up a ramp towards the top of the temple. Our guide explains that this is the Temple of the Moon. Traces of plaster and paint indicates that the temple was plastered smooth and painted yellow to reflect the moon to add to the mystique of the Moon Goddess. There are areas where offerings had been found and an area that seems to have been set aside for feasting. We can look out and see the city buildings rising up all around us and the guide explains that in the ancient days, you'd be able to see clear to the Ocean, so it was a meeting place of both Goddesses. In the original Lima culture, on the seaside they worshipped Mother Ocean and the Moon Goddess, but in the highlands, they had the Sun God and Pachamama, the Earth Goddess.

Most native people lived outside of this sacred space in small adobe huts with flat roofs, because there really isn't any rain to speak of in Lima. The change in architecture really stands out to me, since we had been in the jungle all week, always seeing steep thatched roofs. Although it's a relatively moist climate because of being by the sea, it actually is a desert that needed irrigation canals to water the farmer's fields and to provide water to the sea-side temple.

We walk around the back of the temple where there is a living display of the ancient Lima farming techniques. Archeologists working there have discovered, "remains of alpacas, guinea pigs, ducks, fish and other mollusks, corn, pumpkins, beans and fruits like cherimoya, lúcuma, pacae, guayaba." So they have a current reconstruction of what the ancient farming areas would have been like. Raised rows with the bean plants set down in the furrows allows the plants to retain water better. There are plantings of corn, and what looks like bush beans. Alongside of that in little mud-brick pens are guinea pigs that were traditionally raised for food. There are wooden mangers with greenery to feed the large rodents, and replicas of the ancient stone troughs that hold their water. Next to that, are alpaca in one large pen with the same feeding arrangement.

When the conquering Wari came along, this sacred space was used as a burial ground for their royalty. The area is still being extensively studied and we catch sight of several archeologists working away. Some of the temple has been reconstructed with new sun-dried brick to illustrate better what it would have looked like. They have also added lights around the ruins to dramatically light it at night.

Our guide leads us in a circle, back out to the little museum where we started. Looking at the time, we scamper off back to the hotel playing a real-life game of "Frogger" across the streets.

I tell the lady at the front desk that Mariela from "Local Peruvian Friend" will

be meeting us. We run upstairs, quick
refill our water bottles with the safe water
in the hotel and get downstairs just in
time to meet our new guide, Mariela, a
lovely petite woman with dark eyes and
dark wavy hair. Coriander takes charge of
getting our bags loaded in the car, while I
check out of our lovely little oasis hotel.

Off we go with Mariela who will be guiding
us around for the next eight hours. She
introduces us to Roberto, our driver, a tall
and imposing hispanic man in a suit and a
crisp white shirt. Mariela looks even more
petite standing next to him, but both look
rather like corporate business people
straight out of New York City. It looks
strange to me now, after spending a week
with the tanned and weathered tour
guides in the jungle with their hand-me-
down t-shirts and swim trunks.

We had arranged for an 8-hour driving
tour, so Mariela can show us around and
we can keep our suitcases in the car. At
the end of our time, they will conveniently

drop us off at the Lima airport for our flight out. Next up... the ancient ruins of Pachacamac.

Huaca Pucllana

It takes us about an hour to drive to the ancient site outside of Lima. It is fascinating to see the shanty towns that cluster on the sides of the hills. Built out of whatever comes to hand, they are a sea of chaos rising around us. Mariela explains that they still had what we call squatters-rights. If you build someplace, it's yours after five years. The shanty towns are starting to sprawl out over the ancient ruins, so the government erected a fence. It made for a clear line between the clutter of houses and the barrenness of the un-excavated desert around the historic site.

At the time we are visiting Pachacamac they are working on a grand national museum for Peru. I'm sure it will be well worth visiting when it is completed! But for now, that leaves us visiting a temporary one-room museum with replicas. When we first walk in we see a four feet "totem pole" of the god Pachacamac. "Pacha" means "world" and "camac" means to "animate" or "create,"

so this is the "Animator of the World";
the god who controlled fire, disease,
earthquakes, and the beginning of the
world and time. He is a two-faced god,
reminding me of the Roman god, Janus,
who is also a god of beginnings, looking
both forward and backward in time.

He is carved on the top of the "totem
pole," his eyes wide, with a prominent
nose, under which his teeth are bared.
Depending on your mood, you can see him
as growling fiercely at you, or smiling for
the camera. He is topped by a carved
crown. The lobes of his ears are large and
pierced with dramatic plugs indicating his
nobility. His arms are at his sides and his
tunic is carved with fancy patterns and
possibly designs of corn and fish. He has
patterned pants and his toes are carved
almost like a bird's perched on the top of
the decorated pole. Under him are carved
various figures. I can make out a spotted
jaguar, the wings and tail of a bird, a long
creature with zig-zagged triangles down
its back (maybe an iguana?), fierce

animals baring their teeth, and the sinuous form of a snake.

Under this replica, there are examples of the types of offerings that would have been brought for him: a huge conch shell, woven baskets of grain and fruits, and the distinctive "stirrup vessels" with double spouts that merge into one spout at the top, looking like a horse's stirrup that gives it its name. (We get to learn much more about these fascinating vessels later.)

We leave the museum to go out into the monochromatic landscape that makes up Pachacamac. While the sun is beating down, the oceanside temperatures keep it a pretty steady 70 degrees, so it doesn't feel too hot, but it does look like a barren desert with the yellowish sand and ancient crumbling temples made out of the same materials.

We get into the car and Roberto drives us to the first parking area, where we can get out and observe the ruins. The main entrance of the ancient temple is roped off, but we can look into a huge courtyard. At the far end is a wide ramp leading up to what would have been the top of the temple. Next to this temple complex is a high walled avenue that Mariela explains was one of the main roadways into the area, it runs from East to West.

I found it intriguing that the site is centered on two intersecting avenues that line up with the cardinal directions. It's fascinating to me that the sacredness of the four directions, weaves its way through various cultures and throughout time: from the 7,000 year old traditions of Native Americans in North America who created Medicine Wheels oriented to the four directions; to the Great Pyramid of Khufu with its sides aligned to the cardinal points; to the rituals of modern Wicca, where the spirits of the four directions are honored at the beginning and end of each ritual.

This spot was considered sacred and morphed and changed over the centuries depending on what culture had taken it over at the time, but always it was sacred. It started around 200 years CE with the Lima culture (the same ones that built Huaca Pucllana that we saw that morning.) When the Wari culture came conquering up and down the coast, they took it over and installed their god, Pachacamac here.

Over the centuries, the ruling cultures added onto this sacred site, increasing it to fifteen main temples, with ramps, storage rooms, and patios. The Wari culture gave way to the Ichsma, but still the belief continued. While the worship mainly centered on Pachacamac, when the Inca took it over, they didn't want to interfere with this strongly held belief, so they just modified some of the construction and added a few more features, such as a magnificent temple for their sun god, Inti. "Inti" was also recognized as the essential spark of life within the human soul, so many of the concepts were overlapping with the life giving powers of Pachacamac.

We pass the now crumbling pyramid that would have housed the "Creator of the World" Pachacamac. Rising higher than that would have been the Temple of the Sun. The Incas making the non-verbal statement that although Pachacamac was indeed great, Inti, the Sun God was just a little more powerful.

I mull over the importance of this site. The reverence with which this place was held! The fact that there was an actual god who resided in the temple here! People pilgrimaged here from the heights of the Andes and the depths of the jungle to request favors, ask the oracle for guidance, or to receive healing. They all believed that the "God that Animated the World" resided here, but only the priests could ever approach him because if ordinary people were to see him, the world would come to a cataclysmic end, (presumably with fire, pestilence, and earthquakes.) Mariela explained that in order to even put in your request and offer your gifts to the god certain restrictions needed to be followed, such as not eating salt or meat, and abstaining from sex. Pilgrims were housed in two forecourts and weren't even able to access the sacred area in Forecourt Three until they had followed these restrictions for twenty days, and to reach the holiest spot, they must follow it for an entire year!

In the Temple of Pachacamac, in the top chamber would have stood the holy image, which even the priests were screened from the view of the god by a jeweled curtain which they were reported to approach backwards. The priests would approach the god to consult the oracle on behalf of the supplicants. Rulers would often ask the priests to consult the oracle before beginning certain military campaigns.

This came to an end with the arrival of the Spanish in the 1530's. Francisco Pizarro sent his brother, Hernando Pizarro and his men to Pachacamac, and they forced their way into the holiest of holies. When the Spanish broke through the locked door that was studded with crystals, turquoise, corals, and gems, they expected to find lots of treasure but instead, the Spanish account at the time (which is suspect to political spin) reported that it was a dark, dismal place with an idol reeking of blood, at its feet were gold offerings as well as human remains. Hernando Pizarro smashed the idol and tore apart the sacred chamber, "much to the dismay of the natives who realized that their living entity and deity wasn't capable of reasserting himself with a vengeance as expected."

Mariela explained that a priest brought out the post and showed it to the Incan people, who at first were frightened that the world was going to come to its cataclysmic end, and then lost their faith in the god when it didn't happen immediately.

It was suspected that the priests had hidden much of their gold and silver offerings, so the Spanish remained there for a month, still searching for more treasure. They had destroyed the pole of Pachacamac and the Incan ancestral mummies that were worshipped. The Spanish forbid the worship of Pachacamac, decrying it as the trickery of the devil, and forcibly relocated all the residents to work building the city of "Ciudad de los Reyes," (now known as Lima.)

It occurs to me how almost everyone speaks Spanish, and all of our guides have Spanish last names. This abrupt and dramatic destruction of Pachacamac, did bring about the "end of the Incan world," just not as they imagined it.

"So how is it that we still have an image

of Pachacamac?" asks Mariela. She goes on to explain that the carved pole on display was discovered in archaeological explorations in 1938. She tells us a current theory, that perhaps you were a supplicant to Pachacamac and accidentally broke your fast (or couldn't resist a lovely local maiden), then perhaps offerings were given to this duplicate, so as not to anger the actual god by impurities. But it is believed to be a replica of the original Pachacamac figure.

Our driver takes us to the next parking area. We get out and begin the long hike to crest the Temple of Sun. Mariela points out that the temple to Pachacamac was painted mainly red with yellow decorative elements, so to distinguish the Temple of the Sun, they painted it mainly yellow with red designs. The Temple of the Sun rose up on the highest hill which we are now climbing. Stuccoed smooth and then painted with yellow and red murals, it must have been an awe-inspiring sight. I don't think it was topped with plates of gold like the Temple of the Sun in Cuzco was, but that would've been amazing! We crest the top and I face into the ocean breeze. The cool air making the damp tendrils of my hair brush across my face as I look out to the dramatic view of the ocean.

I turn back to look at the wall behind us. Undoubtably the temple rose much higher in the past, the Spanish destruction of the temple and time having taken its toll. I had learned that even with the relatively mild shifting of the seasons here, it was still important that each Winter Solstice the priests relit the sacred fires. Somewhere at the top of this temple, the priests would have emerged in their shining gold crowns, wide necklaces, and golden ear and nose ornaments all sparkling in the morning light. They would stand high above the crowds gathered below. Using a concave silver mirror, the temple virgins would catch the rays of the morning sun. Using its concentrated energy, they would light the new sacred fire from the power of their god, Inti.

The element of fire is a powerful one. It is manifested in the sun and stars, bright burning balls of gas that are so brilliant they reach across billions of miles and billions of years to illuminate our world. We harness that energy to cook our food, power our cars, warm our homes, and push rockets out to explore other planets. The energy of the sun is converted by plants into food for us and other animals. We convert those sources into the energy to fuel our every activity: from walking, to making love, creating children, and creating art. But even before all of this science was known, the power of fire and the light of the sun was a powerful enough source that it was looked upon as a god.

As we descend the circular path around the Temple of the Sun, we can still see the carbon deposits from where the sacred mummies were burned some 400 years prior. We look out to see the ruins of buildings spread below us. We can see one temple with two long lines of regularly spaced stones that indicate that there was a grand processional with columns through the huge courtyard. In my minds eye, I try to picture it filled with the colorful crowds of pilgrims dressed in the various styles throughout the country with a robed and bejeweled priest standing on the ruined crest of the temple. It would have been incredible in its heyday.

Mariela speaks about the problems with the archeology today. Since the site was taken over by the government there is a long process of forms and permission just to excavate, and then everything must be put back the way it was. If they want to excavate and recreate some of the walkways and courtyards, then that takes another set of paperwork and permits.

We can see the intimidating soldiers who have been posted sentry throughout the whole complex. She says that in that courtyard below us, there is evidence of about twenty mummies buried there, but nowadays they won't dig them up out of respect for the dead.

I mention that I had read about some excavations in Siberia where they got a local shaman to intercede with the spirits of the dead, to do a ceremony where they request permission and explain that the excavation has to do with obtaining knowledge and no disrespect is intended. Perhaps if they could get a shaman who follows the same traditions as here, they could do the same. Mariela says that yes, there are still modern practitioners of the ancient religion, but I'm not sure about how much skepticism she views the current practitioners and the subject is dropped.

We catch back up with Roberto, and he drives us to one last spectacular spot, the Acllahuasi, The House of the Chosen Women. Apparently this was reconstructed by an archeologist about 75 years ago and it is an amazing looking site. However, due to a huge earthquake in 2007, it is in a very fragile condition, so it is viewed at a distance.

We stand on a hill opposite the site and look out at its beautifully terraced apartments with the distinctive trapezoidal doors that distinguish Inca architecture. They surround a lovely courtyard with what was probably cultured gardens and sculpted ponds that may have been used for rituals. We can see some high walls that surrounded the place. Mariela explains that young girls were selected at the age of eight to be sequestered here, never seeing their families again. The girls were selected from the nobility or if they were exceptionally beautiful. It was considered a high honor for a family to have a girl selected, but it could also be a risk. Should the girl disgrace her chosen position, the family and indeed many of her village could be executed. There were guards at the House of the Chosen Women, but they were blinded, so that (theoretically) they could not be seduced by the young women's beauty.

For the young lady too, it was sort of a mixed blessing. They had a privileged position, being trained in gentle arts and the service of the temple, becoming a mamacona, (a position rather like a nun or a Roman Vestal Virgin.) They could wind up in the job of manufacturing the elaborate textiles worn by the priests and the mummies of deceased Inca kings, or making the corn beer (chica) that was used as offerings to the Sun God. They could be selected to become the consort of the Inca ruler or other nobility, or they could be accorded the high honor of being ritually sacrificed by strangulation.

In one of the burial places in Pachacamac, eighty women were found strangled, some with the cotton garrote still around their necks, mummified, wrapped in beautifully woven cloth, and buried in stone-lined tombs with exotic funerary offerings from the highlands of the Andes: coca, quinoa, and cayenne pepper (rather than the local offerings buried with other individuals at the site.)

While we are learning all this from Mariela, a large group of school children in uniform come along. They get a short explanation from the teacher in Spanish. A young boy is standing next to me, and his dark eyes turn towards us when he hears us speaking English. He steps forward towards me and offers his hand, saying, "Hello, my name is Marco."
I am delighted at his politeness and reply formally, "Pleased to meet you."
He then adds in Spanish something that I interpret as "That's about as much English as I know." While my mental gears are thrashing to recall in Spanish, "Hola, mi nombre es Patricia," his class gets hustled off, thus losing a great opportunity for learning on both our parts.

Pachacamac

We wrap up our visit to Pachacamac and get back on the road to Lima. On our ride back, we think to ask Mariela about why John F. Kennedy was memorialized in a park in Miraflores. She says that he never visited Peru and wasn't really associated with Peru, except that J.F.K.'s hometown was near a place named Miraflores. Online it states that it was named because of John F. Kennedy's aid to Peru, so I don't know what version is correct, or maybe they both are.

As we enter the city of Lima again, Mariela comments on the traffic and says that drivers are quite aggressive. If we needed any verification of that, her statement is partially drowned out by an angry car honk. While many people would consider the jungle the more dangerous place, I was of a different opinion, the rickety Peruvian bridges felt safe compared to Peruvian traffic. We watch as cars in the far right lane crazily cut across three lanes of traffic because they

have decided they need to turn left NOW.
Roberto is certainly earning his keep!

Mariela suggests a place to stop for lunch
and we treat Roberto and her to a meal.
The prices are incredibly reasonable at
about $10 for a huge plate of food.
Roberto only speaks Spanish, but we have
fun showing them the professional photos
that Coriander had taken and family
pictures (which don't take much
translation.)

We try to convey to Mariela that we like
"odd things" to go look at and explore,
like the Capuchin Crypt in Rome that was
decorated entirely in bones, but I think we
baffle her a bit. Her standard tour covers
the center of Lima, but she thought we
might be interested in their "Chinatown."
When Coriander explains that she has her
professional camera with her, they decide
to have Roberto accompany us, "just in
case." Apparently, it is only in the recent
past that their Chinatown was entirely

renovated, but people still recall the rampant theft and pick-pockets there.

We walk through a market that is a very tame version of the one in Iquitos. It reminds me of Reading Terminal Market in Philadelphia, with booths set up in a large building space; each selling different foods, kitchen utensils, produce, wood crafts or meat. It isn't of much interest to us and we pass right through.

Standing in the Main Plaza of Lima, with its fountain in the center, we look around us. With the classic architecture, it's hard to remember that the plaza was actually designed in 1535 by the conquistador, Francisco Pizarro. He conscripted all those natives that were now out of work at the closed temples of Pachacamac to start building the roads and buildings here.

Fortunately, they removed the gallows that used to be at the center of the square, and replaced it with a fountain.

For being 400 years old, the bronze fountain is in terrific shape! I see no indications of the Spanish bull fights that used to be held here, but the Cathedral of Lima built in 1622, still rises majestically facing out onto the square.

The Cathedral is made of white stone with towers that remind me a lot of the construction and design of City Hall in Philadelphia. Apparently, Francisco Pizarro laid the first stone in the initial adobe construction and carried the first beam. His bones are resting there in an elaborate marble memorial. We don't go in because it is now designated as a museum (except on Sundays when it is used as a church.)

Mariela guides us down some streets that are closed off to traffic to provide a nice walkway to the shops around. It is known as the Jiron de la Union and this also was originally built by Francesco Pizzaro. Only an ornate carved and lattice-work wooden balcony in a very Spanish style, a few

ancient doors and ornate door knockers
hint at its ancient history, otherwise it
looks much like a collection of buildings in
Philadelphia.

Lima's Chinatown is just two blocks, but it
is framed by a large and impressive
entranceway with bright red pillars and a
green tiled roof. We learn that Chinese
food that is made with Peruvian
ingredients is called "chifa" and has
become its own style of cuisine.

Walking in Chinatown, we see the
ubiquitous round red silk lanterns, and
mechanical waving cats, and smell the
deep, exotic incense, but we also pass
someone advertising in Spanish that they
sell Chinese horoscopes. This mishmash
of cultures is fascinating to me. When we
are done there, Roberto seems to feel his
guarding presence isn't necessary any
more and he goes back to wait with the
car.

It is cute seeing the little Peruvian children during our walk through the city. We pass a large group of pigeons gathered on the sidewalk and, of course, the toddler that has escaped from his padre heads straight for them. I smile at the global commonality of children chasing pigeons in cities! I also see a mother carrying a bunch of bags and a 4-year-old boy at her side that is starting to stray. Although they are all speaking Spanish, I could see when she tells him that she needs help carrying her bag, and he runs up to hang on and "help" her. I may not speak Spanish, but as a mom, I'm fluent in "redirection."

As we are walking, we pass an ornate cathedral. Mariela asks if we want to go inside. It is the Basilica of Our Lady of Mercy. A lovely statue of Mary with arms outspread graces a balcony above the main door. This church was also originally founded in the 1500's by the conquistadors. The side altars are carved and ornate, with rich colors and plenty of gilding. Going just inside and turning to the right, we come across a glass case and what we think is an Incorruptible, Santa Fortunata, but I find out later it is just a replica statue. Apparently, the Catholics in South America also revere and put on display the body of saints that miraculously resist decomposition. The real saint's body resides in Moquegua, Peru (and her nails and hair are said to still be growing.) We had been "collecting" pictures of Incorruptibles in Rome, so I was disappointed that we didn't get to add to that.

What is very different to us is that many of the plaster statues of Jesus are wearing wigs of real hair, and are dressed in elaborately embroidered velvet robes with gleaming golden thread. Even the image of Christ being crucified, is garbed in a "skirt" of velvet, with an embroidered chalice and Eucharist, complex vining designs all done in bright gold thread, and edged in golden fringe.

Under the crucifix is a sign, "Prohibido escribir en la pareo." So I'm still trying to figure out if people were writing their prayers on the wall, or like I saw in Rome, people wrote their prayers on pieces of paper and tucked them around the statues, and this church had decided to discourage this tradition.

After we leave the Basilica, Coriander expresses a craving for a cappuccino. (It may have been triggered by the cathedral and nostalgia for Rome.) Mariela guides us to a little coffee shop. It is probably the freshness of the beans grown in Peru, but it is some of the best decaf coffee I've ever had! I miss my opportunity, never thinking that I should bring some of that marvelous coffee back with me! But the day is getting on, so we meet back up with Roberto and go to the last stop on our list, the Larco Museum, the largest, private pre-Columbian art collection in the world.

Lima, Peru

Museo Larco has lovely landscaping and flowering gardens. After we paid our admission, we walk up one ramp and spy a sign pointing in the direction of the Erotic Art Gallery.

"Well, this I've got to see!" I say, as the sign directs us down another ramp into a grassy courtyard with flowering bougainvillea in reds and purples along with ivy cascading all over the walls around us, and other beautiful plantings. Mariela explains that the reason there are ramps there was because the Larco collection was relocated into this old mansion which was built over top of a 7th century pre-Columbian pyramid!

The Erotic Art Gallery is mainly a collection of the distinctive stirrup vessels: the main spout diverging into two "branches" that then converge onto the main container of the vessel which is formed into all kinds of shapes, although there are some other vases, pottery, and containers in the collection. I am intrigued by the huge amount and variety of "offering vessels." The museum signs simply said that the main ceremonies in Peru at this time (around 200 CE) centered on fertility, sacrifice, and the cult of the dead. Offerings of fluids were important and the vessels may have held water, corn beer or other fermented drinks, and sacrificial blood.

Many vessels are shaped like fruits and animals of Peru, but this collection gathered in two large rooms, centers on all erotic images; couples in various sexual positions, animals mating, figures with exaggerated phalluses, penis vessels, etc.

The collector, Rafael Larco had written, "This gallery provides us with a clearer understanding of the world view of the societies of ancient Peru. At the same time, it offers a unique and fascinating opportunity for the study of sexuality, free of our own myths and prejudices."

It's very hard to look at such images and keep a mind "free from our own myths and prejudices." The images of women "french kissing" skeletons, really make me wonder what they were trying to convey. There was a tradition of women following their deceased husband into death, so perhaps it was a representation of that? I ask our tour guide about the depictions of women "french kissing" a skeleton, but she doesn't know. However, I find it noteworthy that even in Peru, they still refer to it as "French" kissing. How'd the French get such a reputation?!

We move on to the main part of the Larco Collection. There is a wonderful chart that was compiled by the original Mr. Larco, to organize which ancient cultures replaced which in the various areas of Peru. He was an amateur archeologist but he drew some conclusions on the native cultures that have later been proved correct.

Moving into a much tamer collection of vessels, I am still curious as to why they would have created so many of these, and if they were used for liquids, there should have been more scientific evidence since they should be able to analyze residues. Doing further research later, I came across some fascinating information. Apparently, many of the vessels were not used for liquids as were commonly supposed, but they actually are fashioned as whistles.

Experimenting with this, people have reported using the sound of several whistles together to produce mind-altering experiences. This effect of a Peruvian Whistling Vessel was first noticed in the 1980's in Pennsylvania by Daniel Statnekov, who spent the rest of his life studying the effect and spreading the word to other energy workers and healers. He made the observation that unlike musical instruments that direct the sound outward, these whistles pointed back towards the person playing them, immersing them in sound.

According to an alternative energy worker, Lyz Cooper, "People who have heard groups of whistles being played report hearing a buzzing sound that seems to come from inside their head and their eardrums are being vibrated. Every sound we hear produces minute vibrations on the surface of the eardrum which in turn are translated into nerve impulses which the brain decodes. The pitches of each vessel are almost identical but the minute differences in pitch produce a psycho-acoustic effect that has been likened to 'sonic ayahuasca'... This phenomenon is the key that unlocks the doorway to other realms."

This sound phenomena is called "binaural beats." In the past fifty years, there's been an increased interest in studying binaural beats because the effect seems to give us access to alternative states of consciousness.

I had come across this phenomenon in the 6,000 year-old Temples of Malta, where a "sound hole" lets a man with a deep enough voice (or any person with a deep enough drum) create standing sound waves throughout the entire structure. Studies have shown that the frequency that would have been generated has been used to provoke trance-like states and healing. The study of this in ancient cultures is called archaeoacoustics.

But according to Jim Carmen, a Peruvian importer, "the vessels are used by contemporary Peruvian shamans to call spirits..." Which would also make sense based on my experiences with the ayahuasca shaman who did his tuneless little whistle to "call the spirits."

Carmen bases this on his knowledge that these whistling vessels (called silbadores) are "still used in modern Peru in shamanic mesas, especially on the north coast and in the Lima area."

Jim Carmen also had an explanation for the shapes of the vessels. He postulates that the figures represented: animals, plants, shamanic or mythic themes is based on the spirit that you wish to call. A silbador shaped like an owl would call the spirit of owls, that would then reside in the vessel.

The Iroquois have a term called "orenda" which is the spiritual energy that is to be found in everything, however, intention can imbue an object with more of that energy. Thus, a vessel shaped like a spectacled owl, used with the intention of calling upon the spirit of the owl and its shamanic connections, would infuse that container with more of that spiritual essence over time.

So putting all these different sources of information together, it seems to me that the original purpose was to "call the spirits," filling the bottles with more and more of the spiritual essence over time.

The psycho-acoustic properties would certainly aid the shaman in being able to be in an alternate mind state to be receptive to the spirits, and also aid the participants to be receptive to the healing energies involved.

It seems the ancient Peruvians may have known a lot more about the emotional effects of sound. There may even have been archaeoacoustic properties built into the pyramids at Pachacamac, but with the destruction that was wrought there and the further erosion over time, we'll never know. However, these effects are being studied at Machu Picchu and other sites that were made out of stone and have survived intact.

Mariela draws our attention to a striking piece of pottery. It is finished in a glossy, ebony glaze inset with mother-of-pearl and turquoise. She explains it incorporates the "trinity" of the Incas: a condor, a jaguar, and an anaconda. These represent the three realms: the Upper

Realm, the Physical Realm, and the Lower or "Inner" Realm. The Upper Realm consists of celestial bodies, including the Milky Way and celestial deities, like the Moon Goddess. The Physical Realm is the physically perceptible world that incorporates people, animals, and plants. The Inner World incorporates the dead, as well as the place of new life, and deities of creation, such as Pachamama. Caves and springs are places that you can connect with this Inner/Lower Realm energy. Part of the job of the priesthood is to make sure these three realms all stay in balance.

We pass elaborately woven tapestries that still hold their vivid color after hundreds of years. On display is a wide assortment of their woven combs, showing different patterns and weaving techniques in the "handle." I am thrilled to spot an ancient example of a "God's Eye," that diamond-shaped craft that I had made out of popsicle sticks and yarn as a kid. Apparently the roots of this tradition go back far further than I had ever known into shamanic tradition.

On display is a cord with knotted string spread out around it like sun rays. This is the quipu. A complex method of keeping track of math, census records, and perhaps even written records. It is not entirely understood because the Spanish considered it part of the Incan idolatry and did their best to eradicate it.

We proceed into a darkened room containing gleaming gold ornaments: crowns, earlobe plugs, nose ornaments, golden chest-plates, and other spectacular pieces that were used to clothe the priests during ritual. These are rare pieces that escaped from the plunder of the conquistadores who melted down any artistic treasures formed of precious metals.

It must have been a impressive sight to see! The priests standing on top of the pyramid, their gold headdresses and ornaments catching the rays of the sun, their voices magnified to reach the supplicants before them.

Many of the nose ornaments are quite huge and elaborate with dangles hanging down. Mariela says this was to distort the priests' voices, adding to the psycho-emotive effect. Since this is an internationally famous museum, under each piece is an explanation written in various languages. I find the name for the nose ornaments in German particularly amusing, as they are called by the very descriptive name of "nasenschmuckstucke." Coriander had expressed before this trip that she might consider getting a nose ring. I tease her in the museum that if she winds up getting one, I will simply have to refer to it as her nasenschmuckstucke.

I am amused when I notice the bathroom signage in the museum. They are marked as male and female with replicas of ancient pottery figurines. The little nude figures make it quite clear which room is which.

The Larco museum website says, "Museums all over the world usually exhibit only 20% of their entire collection, but Museo Larco is one of the few museums in the world that allows its visitors to go into its classified storage area. The opportunity to see 45,000 objects duly arranged, catalogued and classified by culture and theme becomes an extraordinary and unforgettable experience."

And it truly is an extraordinary experience! Rooms and rooms of glass-fronted cabinets displaying the Peruvian vessels grouped according to theme: a cluster of cacao pods, next to that vessels shaped like corn, through the entire selection of foods, then thirty little owl vessels catch my eye, ones shaped like toucans, snakes, and on through the animal kingdom. The next wall is entirely filled with human faces showing many different expressions... really amazing!

I would have spent a lot more time looking around the whole museum, but the time is approaching when we will have to leave for the airport. We make a quick visit to the museum's gift shop. There are little calabash gourd rattles shaped like owls. Feeling my deep connection to the spectacled owl, I purchase a little one drawn in red, black, and tan, rather like the decorated pottery. As an amusing gift for my husband, I get a pack of playing cards featuring 52 pieces of the erotic pottery we had seen. Coriander gets one or two small items and then off we go.

Museo Larco

Lima gave us an unforgettable farewell. Although it is close to eight o'clock at night, it sure seems like "rush hour" traffic. Roberto impresses us once again with his driving skills. The traffic and horns rival that of New York City. We wind up in one large intersection, and although there are stop lights they appear to be ignored, as at least twenty cars and two buses navigate the intersection pointing in twenty-two different directions. I look up at the bus towering next to us to see the commercial bus driver texting on his cell phone through all this! The honking escalates to the level of a cacophonous choir. Somehow we manage to wend our way through it. I'm not sure it was a great idea to give passionate Latinos two-ton vehicles to drive. I remember the traffic in Barcelona, Spain being equally insane. At the end of our journey, Coriander gives Roberto a high-five for his driving skills!

Now it's just a matter of waiting for our flight. We sit down and Coriander slips off her heavy boots and curls up like a kitten on the bench.

Although this trip encompassed only one country, Peru, I feel like we traveled through different worlds. We traveled through the Upper Realm of the gods, climbing the hills of the ancient desert temples dedicated to the Moon Goddess and the Sun God. We traversed the Middle Realm with Lima's modern city and the scavenged city of Iquitos. We descended deep into the watery Lower World of the Amazon, encompassing the lush jungle and the mystical shamanic realm.

Coriander must have noticed my absentminded and far-away expression, as she breaks into my reveries with her observation, "You know... the airport is the only place you can walk around with no shoes, a glazed look on your face, and sleep on the benches and no one judges you." I laugh.

Travel Tips

Travel Tips:

- A month or two before your trip, make sure you check with your doctor to see what vaccinations you need and discuss anti-malarial drugs. Before I traveled, the Center for Disease Control (CDC) had almost run out of the yellow fever vaccination and I got the last one in the area!
- A raincoat or better yet, a lightweight rain poncho will help keep you from getting soaked through with unexpected showers. I'd recommend a green or camouflage one so you don't scare off the wildlife.
- Ziplock or some other sort of waterproof bags to keep your electronics dry.
- You may wish to bring disposable contacts. I wore my glasses and they kept getting steamed up in the humidity. But you'd want disposable because it could be really hard to clean your contacts when your water supply is uncertain.

- Women, avoid sports bras. When you are hot and sweaty, it is practically impossible to peel a tight sport bra on and off! I really wanted a bra with a clasp.
- Mosquito repellant! As heavy-duty as you can get! You'll need to weigh the pros and cons for yourself, but I figured the chance of cancer from the chemicals was way less immediate than diseases from the mosquitos. Spray your clothes down with permethrin. It actually lasts through getting wet and a few washes. So before you pack for your trip, take a day to spray your clothes, let them dry and then pack them. Also bring DEET spray. I'd recommend against rub-on sticks because ours melted in the heat!
- Therapik. Most folks haven't heard of these yet, but it is great! Despite all you do, you will get bug bites and the Therapik uses heat to "cook" the proteins that you are allergic to. It runs on a 9V battery and it will save you from itchy madness.

- Water bag or bottle. I really found myself wishing for the larger capacity Camelback water backpack. In the heat, you drink a lot! But a water bag with a clip was really nice because it folded up when empty and clipped onto you when you wanted your hands free.
- Water purifier. We actually never did use it, but I was really glad that I had it just in case. It's not very large, so I think it's worthwhile to bring. I got one that came with its own water bag, and it could also be used on the Camelbak.
- Bandanas. We found we really needed these to keep the sweat out of our eyes. We could also wet it in the river and cool our wrists and forehead, *and* the natives wanted to trade for them.
- American t-shirts if you wish to barter for Peruvian crafts in the market.
- Waterproof hiking boots and lots of changes of socks. Dry socks will make you very happy.
- A sarong. My own personal preference, but I loved the light weight covering after swimming or a shower.

- I wish I had brought cash to pay the balance of our reservations. They were happy to accept either American or Peruvian money but didn't want to process a credit card.
- "There's an app for that." Look for a smartphone app to convert money for you.
- Bring a tip for your tour guide and gifts for a shaman (tobacco is always appropriate.) I wish now that I had brought a gift for the chief of the Yaguas, but I didn't know I was going to see him at the time, so just a few all-purpose gifts, such as bandanas might be appropriate.

Sources:
Bailey, Tommy. "Ayahuasca: My Journey to Peru to Participate in an 8-Day Ayahuasca Retreat." Free Range Press, Floyd, VA. 2014

Begazo, Alfredo. "The Official List of Birds of Peru." Surbound.
 25/3/2015. 1/12/2015
<http://www.surbound.com/the-official-list-of-birds-of-peru/>

Cabrera, Giorgio Piacenza. "Pachacamac: A Much Needed and Feared Oracle Spirit or an Alternate Pre-Hispanic Perception of the Creator of the World." AP Magazine. Alternate Perceptions Magazine.
25/11/2015
<http://www.apmagazine.info/index.php?option=com_content&view=article&id=306>

Carmen, Jim. "Whistling Vessels in Peruvian North Coast Shamanism." Etsy.
21/7/2008. 3/12/2015

<http://www.ebay.com/gds/Whistling-Vessels-in-Peruvian-North-Coast-Shamanism-/10000000002902683/g.html>

Cooper, Lyz. "Of Earth and Air - A journey into the world of the Peruvian Whistling Vessels." HealthySound. Soundworks. 9/2007. 2/12/2015 <http://www.healthysound.com/articleWhistling.htm>

Howes, David. "Body Decoration and Sensory Symbolism in South America." Senses. The Concordia Sensoria Research Team (CONCERT) Concordia University Montreal Canada. 11/3/2016. <http://www.david-howes.com/senses/Body%20Signs.htm>

Leone, Beth. "Kambo." Kambo Medicina. 2016. 15/6/2016 <http://kambomedicina.com>

Morton, Ella. "Parque Kennedy." Atlas
Obscura. Dylan Thuras & Joshua Foer.
23/11/2015.
<http://www.atlasobscura.com/places/
parque-kennedy>

Perlin, John. "Burning Mirrors." Whole
Earth (Issue #99, Winter 1999)

Spence, Lewis. "The Myths of Mexico and
Peru." (First Rate Publishers 1913) Sacred
Texts. 20/5/2016.
<http://www.sacred-texts.com/nam/
mmp/mmp10.htm>

Statnekov, Daniel. "Current Developments
in the Peruvian Whistling Vessels."
PeruvianWhistles.
22/12/1996. 2/12/2015
<http://www.peruvianwhistles.com>

Statnekov, Daniel. "Animated Earth; a
Story of Peruvian Whistles and
Transformation." (Berkeley, California:
North Atlantic Books 2003)

Taylor, Leslie. "Tropical Plant Database."
Rain-Tree. RainTree. 30/12/2012.
25/11/2015
<http://www.rain-tree.com/
huacapu.htm#.VI3ic4SKxSU>

Tedlock, Barbara, PhD. "The Woman in the
Shaman's Body; Reclaiming the Feminine
in Religion and Medicine." New York.
Bantam Books. January, 2006

Waymire, John. "Plants Used for
Craftwork in The Peruvian Amazon."
BioBio. 28/11/2015
<http://biobio.com/articles/
craftplants.html>

unknown. "Poison Dart Frog." Shamanic
Retreats. 2012. 20/11/2015
<http://www.shamanicretreats.org/
poison-arrow-frog2/>

unknown. "Amazon River." Wikipedia.
Wikipedia. 3/12/2005. 21/11/2015.
<https://en.wikipedia.org/wiki/
Amazon_River>

unknown. "The Adobe Pyramid Pucllana (Juliana)". LimaEasy. Lima Easy. 25/11/2015 <http://www.limaeasy.com/culture-guide/huacas-adobe-pyramids/the-adobe-pyramid-pucllana-juliana>

unknown. "Record Breaking Giant Amazon Water Lily." LivingRainForest. Trust for Sustainable Living. 2002. 1/12/2015. <http://www.livingrainforest.org/about-rainforests/record-breaking-giant-amazon-water-lily/>

unknown. "Religious Monuments of Lima Downtown." Go2Peru. Comercializadora Electrónica de Turismo S.A.C. 1/12/2015 <http://www.go2peru.com/peru_guide/lima/religious_monuments.htm>

unknown. "Permanent Exhibition." Museo Larco; Treasures from Ancient Peru. Museo Larco. 2/12/2015 <http://www.museolarco.org/en/exhibitions/permanent-exhibition/>

unknown. "Inca Mythology." Wikipedia
8/9/2015. 4/12/2015.
<https://en.wikipedia.org/wiki/
Inca_mythology>

Patricia Robin Woodruff is an artist, author and mystic. She divides her time between the artistic mecca of Floyd, VA, and her homestead in the Appalachian mountains of PA, which is a geodesic dome run off of solar power, deep in the woods. She and her husband unschooled their children, work out of their home and travel whenever possible. Follow Robin's blog on creativity at: InnerArtSpirit.Wordpress.com

Coriander Woodruff is a professional photographer and a Millennial (which means she juggles other part time jobs too.) Her eclectic upbringing had her creating two commercial albums of electronica music before she was thirteen years old, and starting her photographic career at sixteen. Her stunning photos and humorous blog can be found at CorianderFocus.com.

Made in the USA
Columbia, SC
31 March 2018